WORLD FOOD Co.

· CREATE THE ·

TASTE OF THE

WORLD

AROUND THE WORLD
IN 100 DISHES

WORLD FOOD Co.

• CREATE THE •

TASTE OF THE

WORLD

AROUND THE WORLD
IN 100 DISHES

This edition published by Parragon Books Ltd in 2015
LOVE FOOD is an imprint of Parragon Books Ltd

Parragon Books Ltd
Chartist House
15–17 Trim Street
Bath BA1 1HA, UK
www.parragon.com/lovefood

ISBN 978-1-4748-2394-4
S43688

Printed in China

Project managed by Faye Lloyd
Written by Beverly Le Blanc
Foreword by Clodagh McKenna
Internal design by Andrew Easton @ Ummagumma
Photography by Mike Cooper
Food Styling by Lincoln Jefferson

PICTURE ACKNOWLEDGEMENTS
The publisher would like to thank the following for
permission to reproduce copyright material:

Getty images pages 8, 9, 10, 11, 12–13, 18–19, 26–27,
32–33, 36–37, 44, 52–53, 54–55, 60–61, 68–69, 74–75,
78–79, 85, 86, 94–95, 96–97, 102–103, 116–117, 120–121,
127, 128, 136–137, 138–139, 144–145, 152–153, 158–159,
162–163, 169, 170, 178–179, 180–181, 186–187, 194–195,
199–200, 204–205

iStockphoto images pages 4, 5, 14, 16, 20, 24, 28–29,
34, 38, 40, 42, 46, 48, 49, 50, 64, 72, 76, 82, 100–101, 108,
110–111, 122, 124, 132, 133, 134, 140, 142, 143, 148–149,
156, 202, 212, 218, 220, 221

Notes for the Reader

This book uses both metric and imperial
measurements. Follow the same units
of measurement throughout; do not
mix metric and imperial. All spoon
measurements are level: teaspoons are
assumed to be 5 ml, and tablespoons
are assumed to be 15 ml. Unless
otherwise stated, milk is assumed to be
full fat, eggs and individual vegetables
are medium, pepper is freshly ground
black pepper and salt is table salt.
Unless otherwise stated, all root
vegetables should be peeled prior to
using.

The times given are an approximate
guide only. Preparation times differ
according to the techniques used by
different people and the cooking times
may also vary from those given.

CONTENTS:

Foreword

My passion for food has taken me around the world. I studied in Paris and New York; I trained and worked as a chef at Ballymaloe in West Cork; I live in Turin in Italy and my work takes me to England, America and Ireland. One of the great joys of so much moving around is getting to dine out in different cities. For me, a city is defined by food, I remember places by taste. When I arrive I seek out the markets, I want to eat where the locals eat and I have to sample the city's signature dish to really get the essence of a place. When I leave all I can think about is getting back to my own kitchen and re-creating the dishes!

You can tell a lot about the character of a city by its restaurants and cafés. In Melbourne the cafés on every corner, buzzing with students and business people, and the exquisite fish restaurants on the sea front equally reflect the confidence and cosmopolitan mix of this sunny city. In London you can bolster yourself with offal dishes in fashionable restaurants using recipes that go back hundreds of years. Here the sense of history is as evident in the food as it is in the walls of the Tower of London.

A city's food gives us a snapshot of its history. When in New York I'm always struck by how each wave of immigrants has stamped its identity on the city's cuisine: Chinatown, Little Italy, the Irish bars and Jewish delis. In Italy each region is fiercely proud of its local produce and the dish that defines it. The local dish defines people's identity as much as dialect or traditional costume.

Food, almost more than photos, can evoke a sense of time and place, bringing back memories of where the dish was originally eaten. When I think of Paris I think of being a student, tucking into sumptuous Croque Monsieur at small cafés along the Seine.

For me Naples will always be about the best pizza I ever ate; the base was thin and crisp and the topping so fresh and the taste so vivid that my taste buds are still in mourning for the last mouthful. Serving tapas always transports me back to the bars in Barcelona: standing with individual dishes of chorizo, anchovies and tortilla, drinking a glass of cold beer and watching the world go by.

The food of each city and how they eat it tells us how the citizens structure their time: mark the celebrations and rituals of their lives. It is sensual and social: a way of preserving tradition and a wonderful way of getting to know and celebrating each other's cultures.

– Clodagh McKenna,
Chef and international food writer

Introduction

This book is a celebration of the best regional food from around the world. It lets you sample the tastes and traditions of what are arguably the top ten culinary cities where food culture is a significant part of the urban mix that makes each area unique.

Unlike country food, traditionally meant to fuel hard physical work and stretch ingredients to feed large numbers, city food gives cooks more scope for innovation and experimentation, updating favourite recipes and making the most of new and unusual local ingredients. As young chefs flock to cities, they bring with them an enthusiasm and a new approach that soon influences other professional and domestic cooks. And, of course, the multiculturalism of cities – especially London, Melbourne, New York and San Francisco – shapes their food traditions.

The influence of city food, eventually affecting what we all eat and cook is illustrated by reflecting on nouvelle cuisine, the French cooking style that put great emphasis on preparing fresh ingredients cooked in a lighter style with stunning presentation. It swept through Paris kitchens in the 1960s and 1970s, eventually being adopted by chefs around the world and reinventing itself as New American Cuisine in the San Francisco area in the 1980s. The emphasis placed by chefs there on using locally sourced, seasonal ingredients as they adapted nouvelle cuisine for American palates helped expand farmers' markets throughout the country, a legacy that continues. As the new-wave cooking style crossed the Pacific, Melbourne chefs were at the forefront, shaking up Australia's food culture to produce what is known as Mod Oz food, injecting a breath of fresh air into the contemporary cooking scene. Now the movement has gone full cycle as young Aussie chefs bring their idea of fusion cooking to European kitchens and beyond.

The joy of preparing city food is the never-ending variety. Even in these days of globalization, the food from each of these cities is unique. Cooks in San Francisco and New York might be American, but it isn't difficult to identify which recipes come from which coast, making the cooks more like distant cousins than sisters and brothers. In Europe, food from Barcelona, Berlin, London, Paris and Rome looks different, tastes different and has evolved out of different traditions, even though they are all major metropolises. Travelling eastwards, cooks in New Delhi, Bangkok and Melbourne borrow from each other and use similar flavourings but still produce uniquely different styles of food.

City food also offers exciting dining experiences. Restaurant meals can be sophisticated and upmarket, or inexpensive and casual. Paris is renowned worldwide for its fine restaurants with their glittering Michelin stars, but all the other cities in this book also offer opportunities for fine dining. And cities as diverse as New York, New Delhi and Bangkok share the tradition of food-on-the-go, be it well-packed sandwiches or street food cooked to order at tiny roadside stalls.

A Culinary Cornucopia

The recipes in this book highlight the quintessential flavours and cooking style of each city. In the United States, for example, New York and San Francisco dominate the food culture of both coasts, but each has its own culinary personality. Both cities have their own way of reflecting the tastes of home brought by the waves of European immigrants in the 19th and 20th centuries. New York became the country's melting pot, but it is the impact of the Eastern Europeans that stands out on menus today in the form of Potato Knishes, Reuben Sandwiches, Bagels and New York Cheesecake. On the Pacific coast, large numbers of Italian dockworkers have left their mark with Cioppino, the American version of Mediterranean seafood stews, and food of various Asian communities, especially the Chinese, is readily available. Stopping to enjoy Dim Sum is a popular San Francisco pastime.

Many European cooks tend to remain more loyal to established traditions, giving modern twists to old favourites. Two notable exceptions, however, occur in Paris, where couscous restaurants are a direct import from former foreign colonies, and London. Modern London is such a multicultural mix that food from most global cuisines is served alongside British favourites, such as Bubble & Squeak, Roast Pork Belly and Spotted Dick with Custard. There has been a seismic change in the variety and quality of food readily available in the past decade as 'pub grub' has been elevated to restaurant standard and TV chefs achieve celebrity status.

Cooks in Berlin cater for hearty appetites with large portions and often devise menus to be enjoyed with a stein of local beer. However, Germans are becoming aware of the need for healthier eating habits and it is now possible to enjoy lighter meals, although vegetarians may have a difficult time finding much choice as pork remains king. The city also offers Turkish, Middle Eastern and Indian choices. In Rome, cooks are guided by the seasons in an almost religious way. Even something as simple as preparing a plate of pasta is guided by the calendar – in summer it will be tossed with chunks of fresh tomato and mozzarella, or served with the lightest imaginable sauce of lemon and tuna; in winter it is more likely to be dressed with oil and garlic, or a black olive sauce.

The tapas culture of Barcelona is one of the city's defining characteristics. For visitors to the city, hopping from tapas bar to tapas bar is an enjoyable way to replace a set meal, but for the locals it just takes the edge off their hunger before their late-hour evening meal. Baby Broad Beans and Chorizo and Tomato-Rubbed Bread are traditional, but modern ideas include Fideuà, similar to the well-known paella, but made with thin noodles instead of rice.

Dining experiences in New Delhi mirror the city's extremes – they can be sublime and sophisticated, or very basic and rough at a subsistence level. You'll find both Hindu and Muslim food with plenty of dishes that reflect the once-great Mughal legacy. For an adventure, go to bustling Chandni Chowk, in Old Delhi, where stalls cooking pakoras, parathas and all types of street food sit alongside those selling jewellery, saris and just about anything else anyone could want.

Street food is also a significant part of the Bangkok dining experience. It is said wherever you are in the city you are never more than 50 metres/55 yards from a restaurant or food stall. This gives you a chance to sample all Thailand's regional specialities, as well as food from China, India, the rest of Asia and many western countries. The other joy for visitors is that you aren't restricted by conventional mealtimes – you can eat round the clock in Bangkok. If time permits, schedule a stop at the numerous open-air markets (tàlàats) to view the dazzling array of produce. Floating markets (tàlaat náat am) along the canals were once a regular sight, but now, alas, only one exists, at Bang Sai, more to satisfy tourist curiosity than local needs. Or take a bus to Damnoen Saduak, about 80 km/50 miles southwest of the capital, to see the largest floating market.

Melbourne is a city that takes its laid-back attitudes to food very seriously. You'll find a choice of eateries wherever you are – from the popular Italian-inspired cafés to Mod Oz traditional, heritage restaurants and endless foreign restaurants – with the St Kilda area offering a bit of everything. The cultural mix of the population inspires plenty of ethnic restaurants and food markets, with Mediterranean, North African, Greek and Asian cuisines on offer.

Basically, city food, wherever you are in the world, has something for everyone. To paraphrase English writer Samuel Johnson (1709–84), when a man is tired of city food, he is tired of eating.

San Francisco

Freshness is the hallmark of cooking in San Francisco. Blessed with a temperate climate and the teeming Pacific ocean, the Bay Area's cooks have an abundance of fruit, vegetables and seafood to choose from, along with splendid wines from nearby vineyards, so perhaps it's no surprise the American farmers' market movement took hold here. And when the large Asian and Mexican populations add their flavourings to indigenous ingredients, San Francisco food takes on a distinctive style. Yet, even with so much choice, the sweet meat of the Dungeness crab remains unsurpassed in popularity. Although it is fished all along the California coast, local cooks have adopted it, and natives and tourists alike flock to Fisherman's Wharf to sample it in traditional dishes such as Cioppino, a hearty seafood stew.

Dim sum

Method

To make the wrappers, put the flour in a bowl, making a well in the centre. Slowly pour in the water, mixing with a wooden spoon until a rough dough forms. Add extra flour, if necessary, to absorb all the water. When cool enough to handle, shape into a soft ball and turn out onto a lightly floured work surface. Knead for 5 minutes, or until smooth and elastic. Shape the dough into a ball, cover and leave to rest for 30 minutes.

Meanwhile, put all the filling ingredients into a bowl including pepper to taste and use your hands to squeeze together until blended. Set aside.

Divide the dough into 14 equal-sized balls and cover those you aren't working with, with a clean cloth. Flatten the balls between your palms, then roll them out into circles about 10 cm/4 inch across. Use an 8-cm/3-inch cutter to cut out circles. Place a teaspoon of filling in each circle and fold the dough to make half moon shapes, pressing to seal the edges.

Heat a large wok with a tight-fitting lid over a high heat. Add a very thin layer of oil and heat. Add the dumplings, flat side down, and fry for 2–3 minutes, moving occasionally to prevent sticking, until golden brown on the bottoms. Do not overcrowd the wok. Pour in the stock, immediately cover the wok and leave to steam for 5 minutes, or until all the liquid has evaporated. Remove one dumpling from the pan and cut in half to check that the filling is cooked through.

Serve at once with the soy sauce.

Ingredients

Makes 14

90 g/3½ oz pork mince

90 g/3½ oz cooked peeled prawns, very finely chopped

4-cm/1½-in piece of carrot, peeled and grated

2 spring onions, white parts only, very finely chopped

1 large garlic clove, very finely chopped

1½ tbsp cornflour

1 tsp grated fresh ginger

2 tsp soy sauce

2 tsp rice vinegar

2 tsp sesame oil

1 tsp hoisin sauce

black pepper

sunflower oil or groundnut oil, for frying

150 ml/5 fl oz chicken stock or vegetable stock, for steaming

soy sauce, for dipping

WRAPPERS

about 150 g/5½ oz plain flour, plus extra for dusting

125 ml/4 fl oz boiling water

Beetroot, fennel & avocado salad with ricotta salata

Ingredients

Serves 4–6

2 avocados, halved, stoned and thinly sliced

2 fennel bulbs, trimmed and thinly sliced

2 golden, striped or ruby cooked beetroot, peeled and thinly sliced

2 tbsp snipped chives

2 tbsp fresh parsley, finely chopped

1 tbsp fresh basil, finely shredded

1 tbsp fresh mint, finely chopped

55 g/2 oz ricotta salata cheese, grated

DRESSING

125 ml/4 fl oz sunflower oil

2 tbsp fresh orange juice

salt and pepper

Method

To make the dressing, put the sunflower oil and orange juice in a large, non-metallic bowl and whisk until blended. Add salt and pepper to taste.

Add the avocado and fennel to the bowl and toss with your hands to coat in the dressing. (At this point the salad can be covered with clingfilm and chilled for up to 4 hours.)

When ready to serve, arrange the beetroot slices on a serving platter or individual plates. Add the herbs to the bowl with the fennel and avocado and toss together. Add the cheese into the bowl and toss again, then mound the salad on top of the beetroot and serve.

Cioppino with focaccia toast

Ingredients

Serves 4–6

25 g/1 oz butter

2 tbsp olive oil

3 large garlic cloves, very finely chopped

2 green peppers, cored, deseeded and chopped

2 large onions, chopped

large pinch saffron threads

400 g/14 oz canned chopped tomatoes

250 ml/9 fl oz dry red wine

2 tbsp tomato purée

3 tbsp lemon juice, plus extra to taste

1 bay leaf

1 tsp fennel seeds

pinch of sugar

Tabasco sauce, to taste

2 cooked crabs, cleaned and cracked into pieces

400g /14 oz live clams, scrubbed

400 g/14 oz live mussels, scrubbed, beards removed

400 g/14 oz raw prawns, peeled and deveined

250 g/9 oz shelled scallops

450 g/1 lb boneless white fish, such as sea bass, cut into large chunks

salt and pepper

8–12 slices rosemary focaccia, toasted and brushed with olive oil, to serve

Method

Melt the butter with the oil in a large flameproof casserole over a medium heat. Add the garlic, peppers and onions and fry for 5 minutes, stirring, or until tender.

Add the saffron, tomatoes, wine, tomato purée, lemon juice, bay leaf, fennel, sugar, and Tabasco sauce and salt and pepper to taste. Bring to the boil, stirring, then reduce the heat to very low, cover and simmer for 1 hour. Adjust the seasoning, adding lemon juice, Tabasco sauce and salt and pepper to taste.

Add the seafood to the broth in the order it needs to be cooked: raw crab needs 10 minutes; sea bass, 4–6 minutes; clams and mussels, 5 minutes; scallops and prawns, 1–2 minutes; and cooked crab just long enough to warm through. Discard any mussels and clams that won't close before cooking.

Discard any unopened clams and mussels and the crab shells. Ladle the cioppino into bowls and serve with the focaccia toast.

Heirloom tomato & artichoke frittata

Method

Heat 2 tablespoons of oil in a 25-cm/10-inch frying pan over a medium heat. Add the leek and stir for 2 minutes. Add the tomatoes and stir for a further 2 minutes. Transfer the vegetables to the eggs using a slotted spoon, then add the artichokes, parsley, cheese, and salt and pepper to taste. Scrape off any bits stuck to the bottom of the pan.

Reheat the pan over a high heat until a splash of water 'dances' on the surface. Add 1 tablespoon of oil to the pan, swirling to coat the side. Pour in the egg mixture and cook gently for 5–6 minutes or until the underside is just set and lightly browned. Use a spatula to loosen the frittata away from the side and base of the pan to allow the uncooked egg to run underneath and prevent the frittata from sticking to the base.

Remove the pan from the heat, cover the frittata with a large, upside-down plate and invert the frittata onto it. Slide the frittata back into the pan, cooked-side up, and cook for a further 2–3 minutes until the underside is lightly browned.

Leave to stand for 2 minutes, then slide the frittata onto a serving plate. Serve warm or at room temperature, cut into wedges.

Ingredients

Serves 4

3–4 tbsp rapeseed oil, olive oil or sunflower oil

1 leek, halved lengthways, thinly sliced and rinsed

2 firm red and/or yellow heirloom tomatoes, peeled, deseeded and chopped

8 large eggs, beaten in a large bowl

4 artichoke hearts in oil, drained and quartered lengthways

2 tbsp chopped fresh parsley

2 tbsp freshly grated Parmesan cheese

salt and pepper

Crab risotto with lemon & parsley

Ingredients

Serves 4

25 g/1 oz butter

2 tbsp mild-flavoured olive oil

1 fennel bulb, trimmed and finely chopped

300 g/10½ oz arborio or other short-grain risotto rice

4 tbsp dry white Vermouth or dry white wine

about 1.2 litres/2 pints fish stock, simmering

450 g/1 lb raw lump crab leg meat

finely grated zest of 2 large lemons

4 tbsp chopped fresh parsley

pinch of cayenne pepper (optional)

salt and pepper

Method

Melt the butter with the oil in a heavy-based saucepan over a medium–high heat. Add the fennel and stir for 5 minutes, or until soft.

Stir in the rice so all the grains are coated in oil. Add the Vermouth, stirring until it evaporates.

Add a ladleful of the hot stock and stir until it is absorbed. Continue adding the stock, ladleful by ladleful, stirring constantly, for 20 minutes.

Stir in the crab, half the lemon zest and half the parsley, then continue adding the stock until the crab is cooked through and the grains are tender but with a slight bite and the risotto is creamy. (You might not need to use all the stock.) Take care not to break up all the chunky pieces of crabmeat.

Stir in the cayenne pepper, if using, and add salt and pepper to taste. Stir in the remaining lemon zest and parsley. Spoon into warmed bowls and serve.

Red wine-braised beef short ribs

Ingredients

Serves 4–6

about 5 tbsp rapeseed or sunflower oil

2 kg/4 lb 8 oz bone-in beef short ribs, cut into 10-cm/4-inch pieces

1 large onion, chopped

1 large carrot, peeled and chopped

1 celery stick, chopped

1 bottle dry red wine, such as California Zinfandel

1 litre/1¾ pints beef stock

1 bouquet garni of parsley, thyme and a bay leaf

4 tbsp butter

700 g/1 lb 9 oz field mushrooms, wiped and thickly sliced

1 tbsp fresh thyme leaves, or ½ tbsp dried thyme leaves

salt and pepper

chopped fresh parsley, to garnish

Method

Preheat the oven to 160°C/325°F/Gas Mark 3. Heat 4 tablespoons of oil in a large flameproof casserole over a medium–high heat. Brown the ribs on all sides in batches, adding more oil if necessary, remove from the casserole, and set aside. Add the onion, carrot and celery to the casserole and fry for 5 minutes, until tender. Spoon off any excess fat. Pour in the wine and stock and bring to the boil.

Reduce the heat and return the ribs to the casserole with the bouquet garni, salt and pepper to taste and enough water to cover. Scrunch a piece of foil on top, cover and return to the boil. Cook in the preheated oven for 1½ hours, until the ribs are just tender. Do not overcook.

Skim the fat from the surface, remove the ribs and strain the liquid. Return the ribs and liquid to the casserole and set aside.

Melt the butter with 1 tablespoon of the oil in a large frying pan. Add the mushrooms and stir for 2 minutes. Add the thyme and salt and pepper to taste, then stir for a further 3 minutes, until the mushrooms give off their liquid.

Stir the mushrooms into the casserole. Place over a medium–high heat and leave to bubble slightly, uncovered, for 45 minutes, until the sauce is reduced and thick. Remove any loose bones. Adjust the seasoning, sprinkle with parsley and serve.

Slow-roasted duck legs

Ingredients

Serves 4

4 duck legs

1 kg/2 lb 4 oz turnips, peeled and cut into large chunks

30 g/1 oz butter

2 tbsp sunflower oil

125 ml/4 fl oz chicken stock or vegetable stock

1½ tbsp soft light brown sugar

900 g/2 lb curly kale, thick central stems removed, chopped and well rinsed

salt and pepper

fresh parsley, chopped, to garnish

Method

Preheat the oven to 150°C/300°F/Gas Mark 2. Heat a large ovenproof frying pan over a high heat. Season the duck legs with salt and pepper, put in the pan, skin-side down, and fry for 3–5 minutes, until brown. Cover the pan with foil and transfer to the preheated oven for 90 minutes, basting once or twice with the rendered fat, until the meat is tender.

When the duck has been cooking for an hour, prepare the turnips. Bring a saucepan of lightly salted water to the boil, add the turnips and cook for 3–5 minutes. Drain and pat dry. Melt the butter with the oil in a large frying pan over a medium–high heat. Add the turnips and fry, turning frequently, for 5–8 minutes until brown on all sides. Add the stock and sugar and bring to the boil, gently stirring, for 10 minutes, or until the liquid reduces to a glaze and the turnips are tender. Season with salt and pepper, sprinkle with parsley and keep warm.

Meanwhile, put the curly kale in a large saucepan of water, bring to the boil and drain. Return to the pan with fresh water, bring to the boil and cook for 5–7 minutes, until tender. Drain well, squeeze out the excess water and set aside.

When the duck legs are cooked, set them aside for 5 minutes and keep warm. Skim off all but 4 tablespoons of the fat and cooking juices and pour into a large frying pan over a medium heat. Add the kale, season with salt and pepper and stir for 3–5 minutes until hot. Serve the duck with the turnips and kale.

Muscat-poached pears

Method

Cut a sheet of baking paper in a circle the same diameter as a heavy-based saucepan large enough to hold the 4 pears. Add the sugar, wine and water to the pan and place over a medium heat, stirring occasionally until the sugar has dissolved.

Meanwhile, peel the pears, leaving the stem intact. Add the pears to the pan and reduce the heat to medium–low. Add the vanilla pod and orange zest, and lay the sheet of baking paper on top. Cover the pan with the lid and leave the pears to poach for 20 minutes, or until tender.

Transfer the pears to a serving bowl using a slotted spoon. Bring the poaching liquid to a rapid boil and boil, without stirring, for 15 minutes, or until reduced and thick.

Serve the pears warm with the hot syrup spooned over and crème fraîche, if using.

Ingredients

Serves 4

150 g/5½ oz sugar

300 ml/10 fl oz California Muscat wine

300 ml/10 fl oz water

4 dessert pears, such as Bartlett or Bosc

1 vanilla pod, split

1 long strip orange zest, white pith removed

crème fraîche, to serve (optional)

Soft-centred chocolate cake

Ingredients

Serves 4

175 g/6 oz butter, plus extra for greasing

100 g/3½ oz caster sugar

175 g/6 oz plain chocolate

3 large eggs

3 large egg yolks

1 tbsp plain flour

mint leaves, to decorate

Method

Grease 4 pudding moulds thoroughly with butter.

Half-fill a small saucepan with water and bring it to simmering point. Place a heatproof bowl over the pan and add the sugar, butter and chocolate. Stir until the butter has melted, then remove from the heat.

Whisk until well-mixed. Add the eggs and egg yolks and whisk them in. Sift in the flour and fold it in.

Pour the mixture into the moulds and put them into the refrigerator for 30 minutes.

Preheat the oven to 220°C/425°F/Gas Mark 7. Put the moulds into the oven and bake for 8–10 minutes, then remove. Leave them to rest, then turn out onto serving plates. Place a couple of mint leaves on the top and scatter a few around.

Meyer lemon pots de crème with raspberry sauce

Ingredients

Makes 4

300 ml/10 fl oz double cream

1 tsp freshly grated Meyer lemon rind

3 large eggs

1 large egg yolk

150 g/5½ oz caster sugar

*125 ml/4 fl oz freshly squeezed
Meyer lemon juice*

RASPBERRY SAUCE

55 g/2 oz raspberries

2 tsp caster sugar

squeeze of lemon juice

Method

Put the cream and lemon rind in a small saucepan and cook over medium heat until small bubbles appear around the edge. Remove the pan from the heat, cover and leave to infuse for 20 minutes.

Preheat the oven to 160°C/325°F/Gas Mark 3. Put the eggs, egg yolk and caster sugar into a large bowl and beat thoroughly. Meanwhile, return the pan of cream and lemon rind to a simmer before pouring in the egg and sugar mixture. Whisk constantly until the sugar dissolves and add in the lemon juice. Remove the pan from the heat and strain the mixture through a nylon sieve into a large jug for easy pouring.

Pour the mixture into four 175-ml/6-fl oz pots de crème, filling to about 5 mm/¼ inch from the top, and place in a small roasting tin. Pour boiling water into the tin, so it reaches halfway up the sides of the pots.

Place the tin in the preheated oven and bake for 30–40 minutes, or until just set. Remove the pots from the tin and leave to cool completely, then cover and chill in the refrigerator for a minimum of 2 hours and up to 24 hours.

To make the sauce, put the raspberries and sugar in a blender and purée until the sugar has dissolved. Add a splash of lemon juice.

Serve the lemon pots with a drizzle of the raspberry sauce on top and the remainder in a serving jug.

NEW YORK

New Yorkers enjoy the world on their plates. Whatever
cuisine you are in the mood to sample, the chances are
it is being prepared somewhere in the five boroughs that
make up New York City. The contribution of generations of
immigrants from all corners of the globe is evident on menus
all around the town. Many dishes, such as the iconic New
York Cheesecake, regarded as 'typically New York' by the
rest of America, have their origins in Eastern Europe. The
city's restaurant culture offers some of the most sophisticated
dining in the United States, as well as the more relaxed, less
expensive delis, with their unbeatable two-fisted sandwiches,
meal-size salads and Clam Chowder, an all-American
favourite. New York cooking definitely offers something
for everyone.

THE REUBEN SANDWICH

Ingredients

Serves 2

2 tbsp margarine, softened

4 slices of rye bread

115–175 g/4–6 oz cooked salt beef, thinly sliced

200 g/7 oz bottled sauerkraut, drained

115 g/4 oz Gruyere cheese, grated

vegetable oil, for frying

pickled gherkins, to serve

thousand island dressing

2 tbsp mayonnaise

2 tbsp ketchup or chilli sauce

150 g/5½ oz green pepper, deseeded and finely chopped

2 tbsp pimiento, finely chopped

2 tbsp pickled gherkins, finely chopped

Method

To make the dressing, mix the ingredients together in a bowl until well blended.

Spread the margarine on one side of each slice of bread and lay margarine-side down. Spread the other sides with 1 tablespoon of the dressing.

Divide the salt beef between 2 slices, tucking in the sides to fit. Divide the sauerkraut and make an even layer on top of the salt beef, before covering with grated cheese. Top with the remaining slices of bread, margarine-side facing up, and press firmly to compress the layers.

Heat the oil in a non-stick griddle pan over a medium–high heat and carefully slide the sandwiches into the pan. Using a fish slice, press down on the tops of the sandwiches. Cook for 3 minutes, or until the undersides are crisp and golden. Carefully turn the sandwiches, press down again, and cook for a further 2 minutes, or until golden, the cheese is melted and the salt beef is hot.

Remove from the heat and transfer the sandwiches to a cutting board. Cut in half and serve with pickled gherkins.

POTATO KNISHES

Method

To make the pastry, put the flour, baking powder and salt into a food processor and pulse to combine. Add the butter and process until fine breadcrumbs form. Spoon in the sour cream and process again until a dough begins to form. Do not allow the dough to form a ball or the pastry will be tough.

Turn out the pastry onto a lightly floured work surface and knead lightly. Form into a ball and flatten into a circular shape. Wrap in clingfilm and refrigerate for at least 2 hours.

To prepare the filling, heat the butter in a frying pan over a medium heat. Add the onions and cook for 15 minutes, or until soft and golden, stirring frequently. Remove from the heat, stir in the potatoes and let cool slightly before adding the egg and salt and pepper to taste. Allow to cool completely.

On a lightly floured work surface, roll out the pastry to about 3 mm/⅛ inch thick. Cut the pastry into 10-cm/4-inch squares and place a tablespoon of the filling in the centre of each. Brush the edges with a little beaten egg and fold the bottom left corner up to the top right corner to form a triangle. Press to seal. Re-roll any pastry scraps and continue forming triangles with the remaining dough and filling. Refrigerate for 30 minutes.

Preheat the oven to 200°C/400°F/Gas Mark 6. Arrange the triangles 2.5 cm/1 inch apart on 2 large non-stick baking trays. Brush each triangle with the beaten egg. Bake in batches for 20 minutes, or until puffed and golden. Cool on a wire rack and serve.

Ingredients

Makes 24

pastry

350 g/12 oz plain flour, sifted

1 tsp baking powder

½ tsp salt

115 g/4 oz unsalted butter, cut into small cubes

125 ml/4 fl oz sour cream

1 egg, beaten

filling

2 tbsp butter or oil

2 onions, finely chopped

2–3 large potatoes, cooked, drained and mashed

1 egg, beaten

salt and pepper

Clam Chowder

Ingredients

Serves 4

900 g/2 lb live clams

4 bacon rashers, chopped

2 tbsp butter

1 onion, chopped

1 tbsp chopped fresh thyme

1 large potato, diced

300 ml/10 fl oz milk

1 bay leaf

375 ml/13 fl oz double cream

1 tbsp chopped fresh parsley

salt and pepper

Method

Scrub the clams and put them into a large saucepan with a splash of water. Cook over a high heat for 3–4 minutes until they open. Discard any that remain closed. Strain, reserving the cooking liquid. Leave until cool enough to handle, reserving 8 for a garnish.

Remove the clams from their shells, chopping them roughly if large, and reserve.

In a clean saucepan, fry the bacon until browned and crisp. Drain on kitchen paper. Add the butter to the same saucepan, and when it has melted, add the onion. Pan-fry for 4–5 minutes until soft but not coloured. Add the thyme and cook briefly before adding the diced potato, reserved clam cooking liquid, milk and bay leaf. Bring to the boil, then reduce the heat and leave to simmer for 10 minutes, or until the potato is just tender.

Discard the bay leaf, then transfer to a food processor and blend until smooth, or push through a sieve into a bowl.

Add the clams, bacon and cream. Simmer for a further 2–3 minutes until heated through. Season to taste with salt and pepper. Stir in the chopped parsley and serve, garnished with the reserved clams in their shells.

BAGELS

Ingredients
Makes 12

1 tbsp easy-blend dried yeast

2 tbsp sugar

3½ tbsp vegetable oil, plus extra for oiling

1 tsp salt

225 ml/8 fl oz warm water

425 g/15 oz plain flour, plus extra for dusting

1 egg, beaten

1 egg, beaten with ¼ tsp salt, for glazing

poppy and sesame seeds, for sprinkling

filling
smoked salmon

cream cheese

Method

Combine the yeast and half the sugar in a small bowl. Heat the remaining sugar, oil, salt and water in a small saucepan for 1–2 minutes, or until warm and the sugar has dissolved. Pour into the yeast mixture, cover with a tea towel and leave to stand for 5–7 minutes, or until the mixture begins to bubble. Put the flour into a food processor and, with the machine running, pour in the yeast mixture, then add the egg and process until a ball of dough forms. Add a little more flour if the dough is sticky – it should be smooth and elastic. Lightly oil a large bowl and add the ball of dough, turning to coat on all sides to prevent a crust from forming. Cover with the tea towel and leave to rise in a warm place for 1½–2 hours, or until doubled in size. Turn out onto a lightly floured work surface. Knead lightly to deflate.

Divide the dough into 12 equal-sized pieces. Roll each into a rope about 18 cm/7 inches long and shape into a ring. Wet one end and press firmly to seal. Arrange on a floured baking tray, cover with the tea towel and leave to rise for 25 minutes, or until doubled in size. Meanwhile, preheat the oven to 200°C/400°F/ Gas Mark 6. Lightly oil 2 large baking trays. Bring a large saucepan of water to the boil. Working in batches, slide a few bagels into the water and cook for 1 minute. Remove with a slotted spoon and drain on paper towels. Arrange the bagels on the baking trays and carefully brush with the egg mixture. Sprinkle half with sesame seeds and the remainder with poppy seeds. Bake for 12–15 minutes, or until golden and shiny. Remove and place on a wire rack to cool slightly. Serve warm with smoked salmon and cream cheese.

BUFFALO WINGS

Ingredients

Makes 12

5 tbsp dark soy sauce

2 tbsp dry sherry

1 tbsp rice vinegar

juice of 1 orange and 5-cm/2-inch strip of orange rind, pith removed

1 tbsp muscovado sugar

1 star anise

1 tsp cornflour, mixed to a paste with 3 tbsp water

1 tbsp finely chopped fresh ginger

1 tsp chilli sauce

1.5 kg/3 lb 5 oz chicken wings

Method

Preheat the oven to 200°C/400°F/Gas Mark 6. Place the soy sauce, sherry, vinegar, orange rind, sugar and star anise into a saucepan, add the juice extracted from the orange and mix well. Bring to the boil over a medium heat, then stir in the cornflour paste. Continue to boil, stirring constantly, for 1 minute, or until thickened.

Remove the saucepan from the heat and stir in the ginger and chilli sauce. Remove and discard the tips from the chicken wings and place the wings in a single layer in an ovenproof dish or roasting tin. Pour the sauce over the wings, turning and stirring to coat.

Bake in the oven for 35–40 minutes, turning and basting with the sauce occasionally, until the chicken is tender and browned and the juices run clear when a skewer is inserted into the thickest part of the meat. Serve either hot or warm.

PIZZA SLICE

Ingredients

Serves 2

for the dough

225 g/8 oz plain flour, plus extra for dusting

1 tsp salt

1 tsp easy-blend dried yeast

1 tbsp olive oil, plus extra for brushing

6 tbsp lukewarm water

for the topping

6 tomatoes, sliced thinly

175 g/6 oz mozzarella cheese, drained and sliced thinly

salt and pepper

2 tbsp shredded fresh basil leaves

2 tbsp olive oil

Method

To make the pizza dough, sift the flour and salt into a bowl and stir in the yeast. Make a well in the centre and pour in the oil and water. Gradually incorporate the dry ingredients into the liquid, using a wooden spoon or floured hands.

Turn out the dough on to a lightly floured surface and knead well for 5 minutes, until smooth and elastic. Return to the clean bowl, cover with lightly oiled clingfilm and set aside to rise in a warm place for about 1 hour, or until doubled in size.

Turn out the dough onto a lightly floured surface and knock back. Knead briefly, then cut it in half and roll out each piece into a round about 5 mm/¼ inch thick. Transfer to a lightly oiled baking sheet and push up the edges with your fingers to form a small rim.

For the topping, arrange the tomato and mozzarella slices alternately over the pizza bases. Season to taste with salt and pepper, sprinkle with the basil and drizzle with the olive oil.

Bake in a preheated oven, 230°C/450°F/Gas Mark 8, for 15–20 minutes, until the crust is crisp and the cheese has melted. Serve immediately.

NEW YORK STRIP STEAK WITH BÉARNAISE SAUCE

Ingredients

Serves 4

*4 New York strip steaks, or entrecôte,
225 g/8 oz each*

1 tbsp olive oil or clarified butter

salt and pepper

sautéed potatoes or chips, to serve

Béarnaise sauce

large bunch tarragon

1 shallot, finely chopped

100 ml/3½ fl oz white wine vinegar

4 peppercorns

2 egg yolks

200 g/7 oz butter, cut into small cubes

Method

Remove the steaks from the fridge 20 minutes before cooking.

To make the béarnaise sauce, remove the most tender leaves of the tarragon, finely chop and set aside. Roughly chop the tougher parts and add them to a small saucepan with the shallot, vinegar and peppercorns and simmer until it has reduced to about 1 tablespoonful. Strain through a sieve into a clean heatproof bowl.

Bring a small saucepan of water to the boil, place the bowl on top, and gently whisk in the egg yolks until the mixture thickens a little. Add the butter a piece at a time and whisk it in until the sauce is thick. Add the chopped tarragon leaves and mix in. Taste and add salt if needed. Turn off the heat and cover to keep warm while you cook the steaks.

Season the steaks with salt and pepper and brush with the oil. Heat a grill pan to high and add the steaks. Cook quickly for 3–4 minutes on each side, check that they are nicely seared, then cover and leave to rest for 2 minutes before serving.

Stir the sauce in case it has separated, then serve the steaks on lightly warmed plates with sauté potatoes and the béarnaise sauce spooned over the top.

FUNNEL CAKES

Ingredients

Makes 4–6

140 g/5 oz plain flour

1 tsp baking powder

½ tsp salt

1 egg, beaten

125 ml/4 fl oz milk

½ tsp vanilla extract

sunflower oil or corn oil, for deep-frying

icing sugar, for dusting

Method

Sift the flour, baking powder and salt into a large bowl and make a well in the centre. Beat the egg with the milk and vanilla extract, then slowly stir it into the dry ingredients until a thick, free-flowing mixture forms.

Meanwhile, heat at least 5 cm/2 inches of oil in a heavy-based frying pan to 190°C/375°F, or until a cube of bread browns in 30 seconds.

Spoon one quarter of the mixture into a funnel, holding a finger over the hole. Allow the batter to fall into the hot oil in a continuous, spiralling circle until 12.5–15-cm/5–6 inches across, or allow it to fall in a haphazard fashion to form a lace-like circle: the mixture will fall to the bottom of the pan and then rise to the surface. Leave to fry for 1–2 minutes until golden brown on the base. Turn carefully using 2 forks or long-handled spoons and fry until golden brown on the other side.

Remove from the oil and drain on folded kitchen paper. Leave to cool for a few seconds, then dust thickly with icing sugar. Serve at once, then repeat until all the mixture has been used.

Vanilla Gelato

Ingredients

Serves 6–8

425 ml/15 fl oz milk

1 vanilla pod

6 egg yolks

125 g/4½ oz caster sugar

Method

Pour the milk into a large heavy-based saucepan, split open the vanilla pod and scrape out the seeds into the milk, then add the whole vanilla pod. Bring almost to the boil then remove from the heat and leave to infuse for 30 minutes. Remove the vanilla pod from the milk.

Put the egg yolks and sugar in a large bowl and whisk together until pale and the mixture leaves a trail when the whisk is lifted. Slowly add the milk, stirring all the time with a wooden spoon.

Strain the mixture into the rinsed-out pan or a double boiler and cook over a low heat for 10–15 minutes, stirring all the time, until the mixture thickens slightly. Do not allow the mixture to boil or it will curdle. Remove the custard from the heat and leave to cool for at least 1 hour, stirring from time to time to prevent a skin from forming.

If using an ice cream machine, churn the mixture in the machine following the manufacturer's instructions. Alternatively, freeze the custard in a freezerproof container, uncovered, for 1–2 hours, or until it begins to set around the edges. Turn the custard into a bowl and stir with a fork or beat in a food processor until smooth. Return to the freezer and repeat the breaking up of the ice crystals every 30 minutes for 2 hours. Return to the freezer until firm or required. Cover the container with a lid for storing.

New York Cheesecake

Ingredients

Serves 10

100 g/3½ oz butter

150 g/5½ oz digestive biscuits, finely crushed

1 tbsp granulated sugar

900 g/2 lb cream cheese

250 g/9 oz caster sugar

2 tbsp plain flour

1 tsp vanilla extract

finely grated zest of 1 orange

finely grated zest of 1 lemon

3 eggs

2 egg yolks

300 ml/10 fl oz double cream

Method

Preheat the oven to 180°C/350°F/Gas Mark 4. Place a small saucepan over a low heat, add the butter and heat until it melts, then remove from the heat, stir in the crushed biscuits and sugar and mix thoroughly. Press the biscuit mixture tightly into the base of a 23-cm/9-inch springform cake tin. Place in the oven and bake for 10 minutes. Remove from the oven and leave to cool on a wire rack.

Increase the oven temperature to 200°C/400°F/Gas Mark 6. In an electric food mixer beat the cheese until creamy, then gradually add the sugar and flour and beat until smooth. Increase the speed and beat in the vanilla extract, orange zest and lemon zest, then beat in the eggs and egg yolks one at a time. Finally, beat in the cream. Scrape any excess from the sides and paddles of the beater into the mixture. It should be light and whippy – beat on a faster setting if you need to.

Butter the sides of the cake tin and pour in the filling. Smooth the top, transfer to the preheated oven and bake for 15 minutes, then reduce the temperature to 100°C/200°F/Gas Mark ¼ and bake for a further 30 minutes. Turn off the oven and leave the cheesecake in it for 2 hours to cool and set. Cover and refrigerate overnight.

Slide a knife around the edge of the cake then unfasten the tin, cut the cheesecake into wedge-shaped slices and serve.

London

England's capital offers a stunning variety of cooking and food, with immigrant communities bringing global flavours that sit comfortably alongside more traditional dishes. In 21st-century London, chicken tikka masala and shish kebabs are as much 'typically' London fare as are classic favourites such as Bubble & Squeak and Fish & Chips. The popularity of gastropubs – slightly cheaper alternatives to restaurants – gives young chefs a chance to showcase their talent and reach celebrity status, while domestic cooks shop at Borough Market, a popular foodie destination, as well as a network of smaller weekly farmers' markets throughout the city. Yet, amidst the fast pace of the modern city, it is still possible to stop for a leisurely afternoon tea, an enduring tradition featuring freshly baked scones.

Full English breakfast

Ingredients

Serves 1

2 good-quality pork sausages

2–3 smoked back bacon rashers

1 egg

1 slice 2-day-old wholemeal bread
(optional)

1 large tomato, halved

vegetable oil, to drizzle

2–3 mushrooms

salt and pepper

Method

Place the sausages under a hot grill and grill for about 15–20 minutes, turning frequently, until they are well browned. Meanwhile, place the bacon rashers in a dry frying pan and fry for 2–4 minutes on each side, depending on how crisp you like your bacon. Remove from the frying pan, leaving all the excess bacon fat, and keep the bacon warm.

Using the same frying pan used for the bacon, break the egg into the pan. Fry for a few seconds until the white sets, then baste with the fat to make sure it is evenly cooked with the white completely set and the yolk remaining soft in the centre. Remove the egg from the pan using a wooden spatula and allow it to rest on a piece of kitchen paper for a second to absorb any excess fat.

Alternatively, if you prefer, using the same frying pan, place the bread in the bacon fat and cook for 1–2 minutes on one side, then turn over and repeat. Do not cook too quickly or the bread will burn. Set aside and keep warm.

The tomato halves can be placed under the hot grill with the sausages. Drizzle with a little oil and season to taste with salt and pepper before grilling for 3–4 minutes. The mushrooms can be grilled with the tomatoes or quickly fried in the frying pan with a little extra oil added. Arrange the sausages, bacon, egg, fried bread (if using), tomato halves and mushrooms on a large hot platter and serve at once.

Kippers

Ingredients

Serves 1

1 kipper

knob of butter

pepper

buttered brown bread and lemon wedges,
to serve

Method

Place the kipper in a frying pan and cover with water.

Bring to the boil, then reduce the heat, cover and simmer gently for about 5 minutes.

Drain on kitchen paper and place on a warm plate with a knob of butter on top and some pepper to taste.

Serve immediately with buttered brown bread and a squeeze of lemon juice.

Fish and chips

Ingredients

Serves 2

vegetable oil, for deep-frying

3 large potatoes, such as Cara or Desirée

2 thick cod or haddock fillets, 175 g/6 oz each

175 g/6 oz self-raising flour, plus extra for dusting

200 ml/7 fl oz cold lager

salt and pepper

tartare sauce, to serve

Method

Heat the oil in a temperature-controlled deep-fat fryer to 120°C/250°F, or in a heavy-based saucepan, checking the temperature with a thermometer, to blanch the chips. Preheat the oven to 150°C/300°F/Gas Mark 2.

Peel the potatoes and cut into even-sized chips. Fry for about 8–10 minutes, depending on size, until softened but not coloured. Remove from the oil, drain on kitchen paper and place in a warm dish in the oven. Increase the temperature of the oil to 180–190°C/350–375°F, or until a cube of bread browns in 30 seconds.

Meanwhile, season the fish with salt and pepper and dust it lightly with a little flour.

Make a thick batter by sieving the flour into a bowl with a little salt and whisking in most of the lager. Check the consistency before adding the remainder: it should be very thick like double cream.

Dip one fillet into the batter and allow the batter to coat it thickly. Carefully place the fish in the hot oil, then repeat with the other fillet.

Cook for 8–10 minutes, depending on the thickness of the fish. Turn the fillets over halfway through the cooking time. Remove the fish from the fryer or saucepan, drain and keep warm.

Make sure the oil temperature is still at 180°C/350°F and return the chips to the fryer or saucepan. Cook for a further 2–3 minutes until golden brown and crispy. Drain and season with salt and pepper before serving with the battered fish and tartare sauce.

Steak and kidney pie

Ingredients

Serves 4

butter, for greasing

*450 g/1 lb braising steak, trimmed and
cut into 2.5-cm/1-inch pieces*

*2 lambs' kidneys, cored and cut into 2.5-cm/
1-inch pieces*

55 g/2 oz flour

1 onion, finely chopped

*115 g/4 oz large field mushrooms, sliced
(optional)*

1 tbsp chopped fresh parsley

*300 ml/10 fl oz (approx) stock,
or a mixture of beer and water*

salt and pepper

suet pastry

350 g/12 oz self-raising flour

175 g/6 oz suet

225 ml/8 fl oz cold water

salt and pepper

Method

Grease a 1.2-litre/2-pint pudding basin.

Put the prepared meat into a large plastic bag
with the flour and salt and pepper and shake
well until all the meat is well coated. Add the
onion, mushrooms, if using, and the parsley
and shake again.

Make the suet pastry by mixing the flour,
suet and some salt and pepper together. Add
enough of the cold water to make a soft dough.

Keep a quarter of the dough to one side and
roll the remainder out to form a circle big
enough to line the pudding basin. Line the
basin, making sure that there is a good
1 cm/½ inch hanging over the edge.

Place the meat mixture in the basin and pour in
enough of the stock to cover the meat.

Roll out the remaining pastry to make a lid.
Fold in the edges of the pastry, dampen them
and place the lid on top. Seal firmly in place.

Cover with a piece of greaseproof paper
and then foil, with a pleat to allow for
expansion during cooking, and seal well.
Place in a steamer or large saucepan half-filled
with boiling water. Simmer the pudding
for 4–5 hours, topping up the water from
time to time.

Remove the basin from the steamer and take off
the coverings. Wrap a clean cloth around the
basin and serve at the table.

Bubble and squeak

Ingredients

Serves 2–3

450 g/1 lb green cabbage

1 onion, thinly sliced

4 tbsp olive oil

salt and pepper

mashed potato

450 g/1 lb floury potatoes, such as King Edwards,
Maris Piper or Desirée, peeled and cut into chunks

55 g/2 oz butter

3 tbsp hot milk

salt and pepper

Method

To make the mashed potato, cook the potatoes
in a large saucepan of boiling salted water for
15–20 minutes. Drain well and mash with a
potato masher until smooth. Season with salt
and pepper, add the butter and milk and
stir well.

Cut the cabbage into quarters, remove the centre
stalk and shred the leaves finely.

In a large frying pan, fry the onion in half the oil
until soft. Add the cabbage to the pan and stir-
fry for 2–3 minutes until softened. Season with
salt and pepper, add the mashed potato and mix
together well.

Press the mixture firmly into the frying pan and
allow to cook over a high heat for 4–5 minutes
so that the base is crispy. Place a plate over the
frying pan and invert the pan so that the potato
cake falls onto the plate. Add the remaining oil
to the pan, reheat and slip the cake back into the
pan with the uncooked side down.

Continue to cook for a further 5 minutes until
the bottom is crispy. Turn out onto a hot plate
and cut into wedges for serving. Serve at once.

Cauliflower cheese

Method

Cook the cauliflower in a saucepan of boiling salted water for 4–5 minutes. It should still be firm. Drain, place in a hot 1.4-litre/2½-pint gratin dish and keep warm.

Melt the butter in the rinsed-out saucepan over a medium heat and stir in the flour. Cook for 1 minute, stirring continuously.

Remove from the heat and stir in the milk gradually until you have a smooth consistency.

Return to a low heat and continue to stir while the sauce comes to the boil and thickens. Reduce the heat and simmer gently, stirring constantly, for about 3 minutes until the sauce is creamy and smooth.

Remove from the heat and stir in the Cheddar cheese and a good grating of the nutmeg. Taste and season well with salt and pepper.

Pour the hot sauce over the cauliflower, top with the Parmesan and place under a hot grill to brown. Serve immediately.

Ingredients

Serves 4

1 cauliflower, trimmed and cut into florets (675 g/1 lb 8 oz prepared weight)

40 g/1½ oz butter

40 g/1½ oz plain flour

450 ml/16 fl oz milk

115 g/4 oz Cheddar cheese, finely grated

whole nutmeg, for grating

1 tbsp grated Parmesan cheese

salt and pepper

Roast pork belly

Ingredients

Serves 4

15 dried bay leaves

5 x 2.5-cm/1-inch pieces of fresh ginger, grated

15 garlic cloves, peeled and roughly chopped

100 ml/3½ fl oz olive oil

½ tsp pepper

2 tsp salt

1 tbsp whole star anise (optional)

1 tbsp whole cardamon seeds, cracked (optional)

3 kg/6 lb 8 oz pork belly, complete with skin and bones (make sure there are 8 ribs), skin scored with a knife every 1 cm/½ inch or so

Method

Combine all of the ingredients, except the pork, in a small food processor or large pestle and mortar and mash until a thick paste forms. Put the pork belly into a roasting tin that will fit in your fridge, then rub the paste into it on all sides, making sure you get some into the cuts through the fat. Place in the refrigerator for at least 1 hour and up to 2 days.

Preheat the oven to 160°C/325°F/ Gas Mark 3. Place the pork, uncovered, in the oven and roast for 2 hours. Increase the oven temperature to 240°C/475°F/ Gas Mark 9 and cook for a further 20–30 minutes to crisp the skin, checking every 10 minutes to make sure that the pork doesn't burn.

If the pork skin hasn't turned into good crackling by now, heat the grill to high and place the pork under the grill, making sure that it doesn't burn. Cut off the crackling in one large piece and set aside, uncovered. Cover the meat with foil and leave to rest for 15 minutes before serving. Cut it at the table, giving each person a whole rib and a chunk of crackling.

Sticky toffee pudding

Ingredients

Serves 4

200 g/7 oz stoned dates, finely chopped

1 tsp bicarbonate of soda

200 ml/7 fl oz water

150 g/5½ oz butter, plus extra for greasing

200 g/7 oz golden caster sugar

2 eggs

1 tsp vanilla extract

250 g/9 oz self-raising flour

sauce

150 g/5½ oz dark muscovado sugar

25 g/1 oz butter, cut into chunks

50 ml/2 fl oz double cream

Method

Preheat the oven to 180°C/350°F/Gas Mark 4. Put the dates, bicarbonate of soda and water in a saucepan and simmer for 5 minutes until the dates are soft. Set aside.

Beat the butter with the golden caster sugar until it's light and fluffy, then beat in the eggs, vanilla extract and flour, then the dates and their cooking liquid. Grease a 20-cm/8-inch round cake tin or baking dish with a little butter and add the mixture. Cook for about 35 minutes, checking after 20 minutes that it isn't burning. It is ready when a knife inserted into the centre comes out clean. It must not dry out.

Meanwhile, to make the sauce, put the muscovado sugar, butter and cream into a saucepan and stir over a low heat until fully mixed. Increase the heat and boil for 1 minute to thicken. Remove from the heat and keep warm. To serve, place a piece of sponge on each of 4 plates and top with the sauce.

Scones

Ingredients
Makes 10–12

450 g/1 lb plain flour, plus extra for dusting

½ tsp salt

2 tsp baking powder

55 g/2 oz butter

2 tbsp caster sugar

250 ml/9 fl oz milk

3 tbsp milk, for glazing

strawberry jam and clotted cream, to serve

Method
Preheat the oven to 220°C/425°F/ Gas Mark 7.

Sift the flour, salt and baking powder into a bowl. Rub in the butter until the mixture resembles breadcrumbs. Stir in the sugar.

Make a well in the centre and pour in the milk. Stir in using a round-bladed knife and make a soft dough.

Turn the mixture onto a floured surface and lightly flatten the dough until it is of an even thickness, about 1 cm/½ inch. Don't be heavy-handed – scones need a light touch.

Use a 6-cm/2½-inch pastry cutter to cut out the scones and place on the baking tray.

Glaze with a little milk and bake for 10–12 minutes, until golden and well risen.

Cool on a wire rack and serve freshly baked with strawberry jam and clotted cream.

Spotted dick with custard

Ingredients

Serves 6

225 g/8 oz self-raising flour, plus
extra for dusting

115 g/4 oz suet

55 g/2 oz caster sugar

140 g/5 oz currants or raisins

grated rind of 1 lemon

150–175 ml/5–6 fl oz milk

2 tsp melted butter, for greasing

custard

425 ml/15 fl oz single cream

5 egg yolks

3 tbsp caster sugar

½ tsp vanilla extract

1 tsp cornflour (optional)

Method

Mix together the flour, suet, sugar, currants and lemon rind in a mixing bowl.

Pour in the milk and stir together to give a fairly soft dough.

Turn out onto a floured surface and roll into a cylinder. Wrap in greaseproof paper that has been well buttered and seal the ends, allowing room for the pudding to rise. Overwrap with foil and place in a steamer over a saucepan of boiling water.

Steam for about 1–1½ hours, checking the water level in the saucepan from time to time.

To make the custard, heat the cream in a small saucepan just to boiling point. Cream together the egg yolks, sugar and vanilla extract in a measuring jug. You can add the cornflour to this cold egg yolk mixture to ensure the sauce does not separate. Pour the hot cream into the jug, stirring all the time. Return the mixture to the saucepan.

Heat the custard very gently, stirring constantly, until the sauce has just thickened, then remove from the heat. Alternatively, you can cook the custard in a bowl over a saucepan of simmering water to prevent overcooking.

Remove the pudding from the steamer and unwrap. Place on a hot plate and cut into thick slices. Serve with lots of custard.

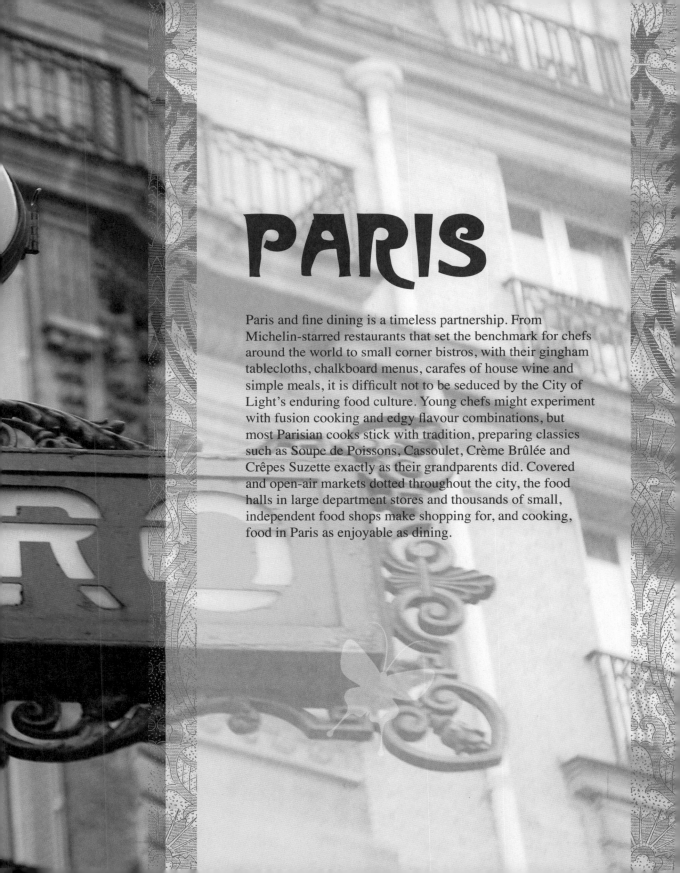

PARIS

Paris and fine dining is a timeless partnership. From Michelin-starred restaurants that set the benchmark for chefs around the world to small corner bistros, with their gingham tablecloths, chalkboard menus, carafes of house wine and simple meals, it is difficult not to be seduced by the City of Light's enduring food culture. Young chefs might experiment with fusion cooking and edgy flavour combinations, but most Parisian cooks stick with tradition, preparing classics such as Soupe de Poissons, Cassoulet, Crème Brûlée and Crêpes Suzette exactly as their grandparents did. Covered and open-air markets dotted throughout the city, the food halls in large department stores and thousands of small, independent food shops make shopping for, and cooking, food in Paris as enjoyable as dining.

SOUPE DE POISSONS WITH ROUILLE

Ingredients

Serves 6–8

100 ml/3½ fl oz olive oil

3 onions, roughly chopped

3 carrots, roughly chopped

3 celery sticks, roughly chopped

1 fennel bulb, finely chopped

6 garlic cloves, roughly chopped

1 bay leaf

150 ml/5 fl oz Vermouth

2 sprigs thyme

1 kg/2 lb 4 oz whole white fish, such as sea bass, Conger eel, skate or pollack, gutted and filleted, but bones reserved

2 kg/4 lb 8 oz bones from white fish or shellfish (ask your fishmonger)

250 g/9 oz unpeeled prawns

2.5 litres/4½ pints water

juice and zest of 1 orange

pinch of saffron

toasted slices of baguette and grated Parmesan cheese, to serve

Rouille

25 g/1 oz fresh breadcrumbs soaked in 1 tsbp water

3 garlic cloves, roughly chopped

1 egg yolk

1 red chilli, deseeded and chopped

½ tsp salt

200 ml/7 fl oz olive oil

Method

Place a large saucepan over a medium heat and add the olive oil. Add the onions, carrots, celery, fennel, garlic and bay leaf and cook gently for 20 minutes until soft. Add the Vermouth and thyme and simmer for 2 minutes.

Add the fish, fish bones and prawns and increase the heat. Cook, stirring, for 5 minutes, then add the water, orange juice and zest and saffron. Bring to the boil and simmer for 45 minutes.

Meanwhile, make the rouille. Put all of the ingredients, except the olive oil, into a food processor and blend to a paste. Keep blending and add the olive oil in a slow stream until the consistency is that of a nice thick mayonnaise. Put in the refrigerator to chill.

Crush the bones by liquidizing the soup in batches, or by using a potato masher and hammer in the saucepan. Leave to stand for 20 minutes. Strain through a colander first, then through a fine sieve, then pour into a saucepan. Taste and season and heat again ready to serve.

Serve in bowls with slices of toasted baguette, bowls of rouille and some grated Parmesan cheese to float on the soup.

LEEK AND GOAT'S CHEESE CRÊPES

Ingredients

Makes 8

30 g/1 oz unsalted butter

½ tbsp sunflower oil

200 g/7 oz leeks, halved, rinsed and finely shredded

freshly grated nutmeg, to taste

1 tbsp finely snipped fresh chives

8 savoury crêpes

85 g/3 oz soft goat's cheese, rind removed if necessary, chopped

salt and pepper

Method

Preheat the oven to 200°C/400°F/Gas Mark 6. Melt the butter with the oil in a heavy-based saucepan with a lid over a medium–high heat. Add the leeks and stir around so that they are well coated. Stir in salt and pepper to taste, but remember the cheese might be salty. Add a few gratings of nutmeg, then cover the leeks with a sheet of wet greaseproof paper and put the lid on the saucepan. Reduce the heat to very low and leave the leeks to sweat for 5–7 minutes until tender, but not brown. Stir in the chives, then taste and adjust the seasoning if necessary.

Put 1 crêpe on the work surface and put one eighth of the leeks on the crêpe, top with one eighth of the cheese, then fold the crêpe into a square parcel or simply roll it around the filling. Place the stuffed crêpe on a baking tray, then continue to fill and fold or roll the remaining crêpes.

Put the baking tray in the oven and bake for 5 minutes, or until the crêpes are hot and the cheese starts to melt. Serve hot.

RILLETS

Ingredients

Makes about 1.5 kg/3 lb 5 oz

500 g/1 lb 2 oz pork shoulder

1 kg/2 lb 4 oz pork belly, rindless and boneless

300 g/10½ oz pork fat or lard

500 ml/18 fl oz water

1 bouquet garni of 2 sprigs thyme, 2 sprigs parsley and 3 bay leaves, tied with string

1 clove

½ tsp mixed spice

grating of nutmeg

salt and pepper

to serve

gherkins

mustard

crusty bread

Method

Cut the meat into 5-cm/2-inch cubes, and chop the fat into 1-cm/½-inch cubes. Place the meat and fat in a large heavy-based saucepan with the water, bouquet garni and clove. (Don't be tempted to add any more water – this method is a sort of gentle steaming. The pork should collapse, not boil).

Cover the pan and place it over the lowest heat your hob can create, using a heat diffuser if you've got one, or place it into a very slow oven, 120°C/250°F/Gas Mark ½. The pot should just be gently shuddering.

Cook for 4–6 hours, checking and stirring about every 30 minutes to make sure that it's not burning.

Remove from the heat and set aside to cool. Remove the bouquet garni and clove. While it's still slightly warm add the spices and seasonings, then take two forks and gently tear apart the pork, mixing the fat with the meat. Be careful to keep the 'planks' texture and avoid turning the meat into a paste.

Cover the meat with a piece of greased paper or clingfilm and refrigerate for 2–3 days before serving (although you could eat them straight away). They will last for at least a further week in the refrigerator, but if you put them into sterilized jars and spread a layer of melted lard on top, they will keep for months.

To serve, drop a spoonful onto a plate beside some gherkins, mustard and crusty bread.

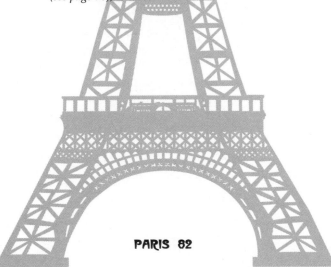

BOUILLABAISSE

Ingredients

Serves 8

1 kg/2 lb 4 oz selection of at least 4 different firm white fish fillets, such as red mullet, snapper, sea bass, eel or monkfish, scaled and cleaned, but not skinned

100 ml/3½ fl oz olive oil

2 onions, finely chopped

1 fennel bulb, finely chopped

4 garlic cloves, crushed

1.2 kg/2 lb 6 oz canned chopped plum tomatoes

1.5 litres/2¾ pints fish stock

pinch saffron strands

grated zest of 1 orange

bouquet garni of 2 sprigs thyme, 2 sprigs parsley and 2 bay leaves, tied together with string

500 g/1 lb 2 oz mussels, cleaned

500 g/1 lb 2 oz cooked prawns, shell-on

salt and pepper

crusty French baguette and Rouille (see page 76), to serve

Method

Carefully pin-bone the fish, then cut the fillets into bite-sized pieces.

Heat the olive oil in a very large frying pan or wide saucepan with a lid and gently fry the onion and fennel for about 15 minutes until soft. Add the garlic and fry for 2 minutes, then add the tomatoes and simmer for 2 minutes. Add the stock, saffron, orange zest and bouquet garni and bring to the boil. Simmer, uncovered, for 15 minutes.

Add the fish pieces, mussels and prawns and cover the pan. Simmer for a further 5–10 minutes, until the mussels have opened. Discard any that remain closed. Check the seasoning.

Serve with some crusty baguette and rouille.

CROQUE MONSIEUR

Method

Preheat the grill to high. Lay one piece of bread buttered side up and place the ham on top. Cover with two thirds of the cheese and season. Lay the other slice of bread on top, buttered side down. Brush the top side with the melted butter and place the bread, buttered side up, under the grill.

Grill until browned, then remove. Turn the sandwich over and scatter the remaining cheese on top. Replace under the grill and cook until the cheese is bubbling and browned. Remove and serve with a green salad.

Ingredients

Serves 1

2 slices white bread, buttered

2 slices smoked ham

55 g/2 oz Gruyère cheese, grated

knob of butter, melted

salt and pepper

lightly dressed mixed green salad, to serve

RATATOUILLE

Ingredients

Serves 4

3 red peppers

200 ml/7 fl oz olive oil

250 g/9 oz courgettes, thickly sliced

1 fennel bulb, roughly chopped

2 large red onions, roughly sliced

3 white onions, thickly sliced

2 large aubergines, thickly sliced

600 g/1 lb 5 oz ripe tomatoes, blanched, peeled, cored and deseeded

1 large tbsp fresh thyme leaves

1 large tbsp fresh rosemary leaves

1 tsp sugar

salt and pepper

crusty bread and butter, to serve

Method

Preheat the grill to high, then place the red peppers on the grill tray and place under the heat until the skin blackens. Turn and grill again, continuing until they are blackened all over. Put them in a bowl and cover with clingfilm to sweat for 10 minutes, then peel them under cold running water. Cut them open and deseed them, then chop the flesh into large chunks.

Meanwhile, place a large heavy-based saucepan over a medium heat and add half the oil. Add the courgettes and fry until they begin to brown. Transfer them to a large roasting tin and keep warm. Add the fennel and onions to the pan and fry for 15–20 minutes until they soften, then transfer them to the roasting tin. Add the aubergines and some more oil (they will soak up a lot) and fry until they begin to brown. Add them to the roasting tin, laid flat in a single layer.

Preheat the oven to 190°C/375°F/Gas Mark 5. Add the tomatoes, red peppers, thyme and rosemary to the roasting tin and distribute the vegetables evenly across it. Sprinkle the sugar over the whole lot and gently mix through. There should be one layer of vegetables, not a stew. If you need more room, use two roasting tins. Season with salt and pepper, drizzle with olive oil and place, uncovered, in the preheated oven for 40–50 minutes until they start to brown.

Refrigerate overnight or eat immediately with crusty bread and butter.

CASSOULET

Method

Drain and rinse the beans and put them in a large saucepan with the bouquet garni, celery, onion quarters, whole garlic and seasoning. Add the water and bring to the boil. Skim off any foam, then reduce the heat to low. Gently simmer for 1 hour, uncovered.

Meanwhile, cut the meat into pieces 4 cm/ 1½ inches square, then add the duck fat to a large heavy-based saucepan and put over a high heat. Add the pork belly and brown it all over. Remove and reserve, then repeat with the sausage, then the lamb. Add the sliced onions, chopped garlic and tomato purée and cook in the remaining fat for 2 minutes. Remove from the heat and leave to cool.

Preheat the oven to 180°C/350°F/Gas Mark 4. Drain the beans, reserving the liquid but discarding the vegetables. In a large casserole, layer beans and meat alternately until they're all used up. Add the fried garlic, onion and tomato purée mixture and enough of the bean-cooking liquid to almost cover the beans. Sprinkle over the breadcrumbs and cook in the oven, covered, for 1 hour. Reduce the heat to 140°C/275°F/ Gas Mark 1, remove the cover and cook for a further hour.

Check that it's not too dry, adding a little heated bean liquid or water if necessary. Stir the crust into the top of the cassoulet and serve with a green salad.

Ingredients

Serves 8

500 g/1 lb 2 oz dried haricot beans, soaked overnight

bouquet garni of 4 sprigs parsley, 2 sprigs thyme and 4 bay leaves, tied with string

1 celery stick, roughly chopped

3 onions, 1 quartered, 2 thinly sliced

4 large garlic cloves, 2 whole, 2 chopped

2 litres/3½ pints water

500 g/1 lb 2 oz pork belly, skin removed and meat cut into 4 large chunks

2 tbsp duck fat or vegetable oil

400 g/14 oz Toulouse or pork sausage, sliced

400 g/14 oz lamb shoulder, boned and cut into 4 large chunks

2 tbsp tomato purée

150 g/5½ oz fresh breadcrumbs

salt and pepper

fresh green salad, to serve

CRÈME BRÛLÉE

Ingredients

Serves 8

500 ml/18 fl oz double cream

1 vanilla pod

100 g/3½ oz caster sugar, plus extra for the topping

6 egg yolks

Method

Preheat the oven to 160°C/325°F/Gas Mark 3.

Pour the cream into a small saucepan. Split the vanilla pod in half lengthways. Scrape the seeds into the pan, then chop the pod into little pieces and add that too. Heat the cream to boiling, then reduce the heat and simmer gently for 5 minutes.

Put the sugar and egg yolks in a heatproof bowl and beat with a spoon until well mixed. Pour the hot cream into the egg mixture, beating (not whisking) as you pour, until it's nicely thickened. Pass this custard through a fine sieve into another bowl or jug. Pour the mixture into a wide, flat dish (or 8 small shallow dishes) and lay this in a roasting tray. Boil a kettle and carefully pour the hot water into the tray so that it comes halfway up the sides of the crème brûlée dish or dishes.

Place in the preheated oven and bake for about 33–45 minutes until the custard has just set.

Remove from the oven and leave to cool to room temperature. Sprinkle some caster sugar over the custard and then gently caramelize it using a kitchen blow torch, or under a very hot grill. Leave to cool for a few minutes then serve.

CRÊPE SUZETTE

Ingredients

Serves 4

8 sweet crêpes

2 tbsp brandy

orange sauce

55 g/2 oz caster sugar

1 tbsp water

finely grated rind of 1 large orange

125 ml/4 fl oz freshly squeezed orange juice

55 g/2 oz unsalted butter, diced

1 tbsp Cointreau, Grand Marnier or other orange-flavoured liqueur

Method

To make the orange sauce, place the sugar in a wide sauté or frying pan over a medium heat and stir in the water. Continue stirring until the sugar dissolves, then increase the heat to high and leave the syrup to bubble for 1–2 minutes until it just begins to turn golden brown.

Stir in the orange rind and juice, then add the butter and continue stirring until it melts. Stir in the orange-flavoured liqueur.

Lay one of the crêpes flat in the sauté pan and spoon the sauce over. Using a fork and the spoon, fold the crêpe into quarters and push to the side of the pan. Add the next crêpe to the pan and repeat. Continue until all the crêpes are coated with the sauce and folded. Remove the pan from the heat.

Warm the brandy in a ladle or small saucepan, ignite and pour it over the crêpes to flambé, shaking the sauté pan.

When the flames die down, serve the crêpes with the sauce spooned over.

TARTE TATIN

Method

Place a 20-cm/8-inch ovenproof frying pan over a low heat and add the sugar. Melt the sugar until it starts to caramelize, but do not let it burn, then add the butter and stir it in to make a light toffee sauce. Remove from the heat.

Peel the apples and cut them into eighths vertically. Core the apples and lay them in the pan on top of the toffee sauce, cut side up. They should fill the pan. If there are any large gaps, add a few more apple pieces. Put the pan over a medium heat and cover. Simmer, without stirring, for about 5–10 minutes until the apples have soaked up some of the sauce, then remove from the heat.

Preheat the oven to 190°C/375°F/Gas Mark 5. Roll out the pastry so that it will thickly cover the pan, with extra over the sides. Lay it on top of the apples and tuck the edges down inside between the fruit and the pan until it is sealed. Don't worry about making it look too neat – it will be turned over before eating.

Put the pan into the preheated oven and bake for 25–35 minutes, checking to make sure the pastry doesn't burn. The pastry should be puffed and golden. Remove from the oven and leave to rest for 30–60 minutes.

When you're ready to eat, make sure the tart is still a little warm (you can reheat it on the hob if need be) and place a plate on top. Carefully turn it over and lift the frying pan off. Serve with some vanilla ice cream.

Ingredients
Serves 6

200 g/7 oz caster sugar

150 g/5½ oz unsalted butter

800 g/1 lb 12 oz Cox or Golden Delicious apples

350 g/12 oz ready-made puff pastry

vanilla ice cream, to serve

ROME

Roman menus are guided by the seasons and tradition.
Simple pasta dishes, grilled meats and fish and fresh
vegetables lightly cooked in olive oil with garlic are the
backbone of la cucina romana, or the Roman kitchen.
Preparing top-quality ingredients with perfect simplicity is
a valued attribute for any Roman cook, be they professional
or domestic. Anyone looking for experimentation and
novelty while dining in the Eternal City will be greatly
disappointed. Instead, Romans take comfort in the
predictable familiarity of mealtimes throughout the year.
In spring, for example, young vegetables are celebrated
with Risotto Primavera, then when the calendar moves on
to summer, Italian Tomato Soup features, giving way to
comforting bowls of Ribollita in winter. Strawberries in
December is simply not the Roman way.

ITALIAN TOMATO SOUP

Ingredients

Serves 6

300 g/10½ oz sourdough bread

100 ml/3½ fl oz chicken stock

4 tbsp extra virgin olive oil

3 tbsp fresh sage leaves, shredded

4 garlic cloves, peeled and finely chopped

800 g/1 lb 12 oz canned peeled plum tomatoes

1 tsp sugar

250 ml/9 fl oz hot water

55 g/2 oz Parmesan cheese, grated

salt and pepper

Method

Chop the bread into rough chunks, about 2.5 cm/1 inch square. Place a heavy-based saucepan over a medium heat. Add the stock, oil and sage and simmer until reduced by half. Add the bread and garlic, increase the heat to high and fry until all the liquid has been soaked up and the bread begins to crisp.

Add the tomatoes and sugar, stir and simmer for 15 minutes. Add up to 250 ml/ 9 fl oz hot water to thin the soup to your preferred consistency (it should be quite thick). Simmer for a further minute. Taste and adjust the seasoning.

Ladle into bowls, sprinkle a little Parmesan cheese on top and serve.

RIBOLLITA

Ingredients

Serves 4

3 tbsp olive oil

2 medium red onions, roughly chopped

3 carrots, sliced

3 celery sticks, roughly chopped

3 garlic cloves, chopped

1 tbsp chopped fresh thyme

400 g/14 oz canned cannellini beans, drained and rinsed

400 g/14 oz canned chopped tomatoes

600 ml/1 pint water or vegetable stock

2 tbsp chopped fresh parsley

500 g/1 lb 2 oz cavolo nero or Savoy cabbage, trimmed and sliced

1 small day-old ciabatta loaf, torn into small pieces

salt and pepper

extra virgin olive oil, to serve

Method

Heat the oil in a large saucepan and cook the onions, carrots and celery for 10–15 minutes, stirring frequently. Add the garlic, thyme, and salt and pepper to taste. Continue to cook for a further 1–2 minutes, until the vegetables are golden and caramelized.

Add the cannellini beans to the pan and pour in the tomatoes. Add enough of the water to cover the vegetables.

Bring to the boil and simmer for 20 minutes. Add the parsley and cavolo nero and cook for a further 5 minutes.

Stir in the bread and add a little more water, if needed. The consistency should be thick.

Taste and adjust the seasoning, if needed. Ladle into warmed serving bowls and serve hot, drizzled with extra virgin olive oil.

TOASTED AUBERGINE & ANCHOVY FOCACCIA WITH GOAT'S CHEESE

Ingredients
Serves 4

*1 thick focaccia loaf (about 15 cm/ 6 inches) or
2 Italian flatbreads*

50 g/2 oz canned anchovies in olive oil

1 aubergine, about 250 g/9 oz, thinly sliced

6 spring onions, chopped

150 g/5½ oz goat's cheese, thinly sliced

handful of basil leaves

handful of fresh coriander leaves

grated rind of 1 lemon

4 tbsp olive oil

10–12 cherry tomatoes, halved

Method

Preheat the grill to a medium–high setting. Slice the bread in half horizontally and lay on the rack in the grill pan. Toast the underside of the bottom layer, and cut side of the top layer, for about 2 minutes, until browned.

Drain and reserve the oil from the anchovies. Remove the bread and lay the aubergine slices on the rack. Brush with the reserved oil and grill for 4–5 minutes, until well browned.

Chop the anchovies and mix with the spring onions. Arrange the aubergines and cheese on the bread, covering the untoasted surfaces of the bottom and the top of the loaf (or the tops of both flatbreads). Top with the anchovy mixture. Brush the remaining oil lightly over the aubergine. Grill for 3–4 minutes, until browned.

Purée the basil, coriander, lemon rind and olive oil in a blender. Top the bottom layer of bread with tomatoes and add the second layer on top, aubergines up. Cut into wedges. Serve drizzled with the herb oil.

SALTIMBOCCA

Method

Lay the pork chops on a board and flatten them with a mallet or rolling pin until they are the same size as the ham slices. Lay down a piece of ham, put a piece of pork on top and place a sage leaf at the edge nearest to you. Season with salt and pepper then roll the meat around the sage leaf and secure it with a cocktail stick. The ham should be on the outside. Repeat with all four chops.

Place a wide, heavy-based saucepan over a high heat. Add the butter and then the meat rolls and brown them quickly on all sides. Add the Marsala and reduce the heat to a simmer. Cover and cook for about 10–15 minutes, until the meat is cooked through. Remove the rolls and keep them warm, and increase the heat and reduce the liquid for 2 minutes to thicken.

Serve the rolls on warmed plates with sautéed potatoes and a green salad and pour over a little of the sauce.

Ingredients

Serves 4

4 pork chops, bones and fat removed

4 large, thin slices Parma ham or San Daniele ham

4 large sage leaves

100 g/3½ oz unsalted butter

200 ml/7 fl oz Marsala, Madeira or dry white wine

salt and pepper

sautéed potatoes and a green salad, to serve

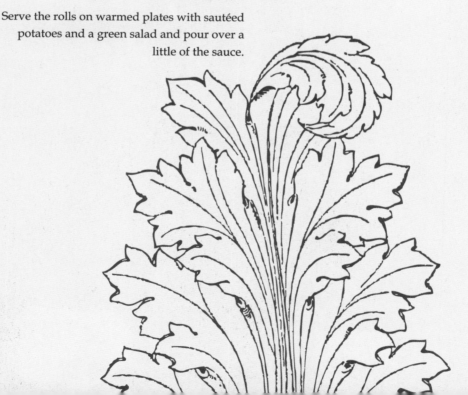

WHOLE ARTICHOKES
WITH LEMON & THYME BUTTER

Ingredients

Serves 4

2 lemons

4 large globe artichokes

250 g/9 oz butter

2 tbsp fresh thyme leaves

zest and juice of 1 lemon

salt and pepper

crusty bread, to serve

Method

Half fill a large saucepan with cold water. Halve the lemons, squeeze the juice into the water and drop the skins in too. Cut the stalks off the artichokes near the base, then 'scalp' them by chopping off the top 2.5 cm/1 inch of the leaves. Add them to the water, cover and bring to the boil. Once boiling, the artichokes will take 20–30 minutes to cook, depending on their tenderness and size. They are ready when the outer leaves can be pulled off without any effort.

Drain the artichokes, turn them upside down and leave to cool for 15 minutes while you make your lemon and thyme butter. Gently melt the butter in a small saucepan, and mix in the thyme, lemon zest and juice and salt and pepper.

Place the artichokes in shallow bowl and season with salt and pepper. Pour the butter into small bowls, either individually or to share. Put a large bowl in the middle of the table for discarded artichoke bits and leaves. Serve with bread for mopping up.

RISOTTO PRIMAVERA

Method

Prepare the green vegetables: pod the peas, chop the asparagus into bite-sized portions, cut the courgettes diagonally into finger-thick slices, top and tail the beans.

Bring a large saucepan of lightly salted water to the boil, add the prepared vegetables and blanch for 1 minute, then remove and drain.

Place a large heavy-based saucepan over a medium heat, add the olive oil and the onions and cook them gently for about 10 minutes until soft. Add the rice and fry, stirring it into the oil for 2 minutes. Reduce the heat, add a ladleful of stock and stir it into the rice. Gradually add more stock as each ladleful is absorbed. Check the rice, it should be slightly hard in the middle (you may need a little more or less of the liquid). Add the last ladle of stock, the Vermouth and the herbs and cook for another 5 minutes.

Add the butter, cheese and blanched vegetables, check for seasoning and heat through, stirring gently.

Serve in warmed bowls, with Parmesan cheese to sprinkle on top.

Ingredients

Serves 4

200 g/7 oz fresh or frozen peas

200 g/7 oz asparagus

200 g/7 oz courgettes

200 g/7 oz French beans

2 tbsp olive oil

1 large onion, finely chopped

250 g/9 oz risotto rice

700 ml/1¼ pints warm chicken stock

3½ tbsp Vermouth or white wine

handful chopped parsley

1 tbsp fresh thyme leaves

75 g/2½ oz butter

125 g/4½ oz grated Parmesan cheese, plus extra to serve

salt and pepper

LINGUINI with CLAMS

Method

Cook the linguini according to the instructions on the packet, drain and toss with a splash of olive oil. Cover and keep warm.

Add half the olive oil to a large saucepan with a lid and place over a high heat. Add the garlic, shallots and chilli and cook gently for 8–10 minutes until soft. Add the wine, bring to the boil and cook for 2 minutes. Add the clams, cover and cook for a further 2–5 minutes, or until all the clams have opened. Discard any clams which remain closed. Add the drained linguini, parsley, lemon zest, the remaining olive oil and some salt and pepper and mix thoroughly.

Serve in warmed bowls, with another bowl for discarded shells.

Ingredients

Serves 2–4

200 g/7 oz dried linguini pasta

3 tbsp extra virgin olive oil

4 garlic cloves, finely chopped

2 shallots, finely chopped

½ fresh red chilli, finely chopped

125 ml/4 fl oz white wine

1 kg/2 lb 4 oz fresh clams, tellines or cockles, cleaned

handful of parsley, chopped

zest of 1 lemon

salt and pepper

ZABAGLIONE

Ingredients

Serves 6

6 egg yolks

70 g/2½ oz caster sugar

175 ml/6 fl oz Marsala, Madeira or other sweet
dessert wine

splash of brandy

amaretti biscuits, to serve

Method

Half-fill a saucepan with water and bring to the boil. Place a heatproof bowl over the saucepan so that it doesn't quite touch the boiling water.

Put the sugar and eggs into the bowl and whisk until light and creamy. Add the Marsala a little at a time, whisking constantly, then add the brandy and continue whisking for up to 15 minutes until you have a floaty, silky foam.

Pour it into bowls and serve with amaretti biscuits. It can also be made ahead of time and served chilled.

PANETTONE BREAD-AND-BUTTER PUDDING

Ingredients

Serves 4–6

100 g/3½ oz raisins, sultanas or chopped dates

4 tbsp brandy

300 ml/10 fl oz milk

450 ml/16 fl oz double cream

1 vanilla pod, split, or 1 tsp vanilla extract

150 g/5½ oz butter, softened, plus extra for greasing

10 medium loaf-sized slices of panettone, preferably chocolate-flavoured, or white bread, crusts removed

4 eggs

150 g/5½ oz caster sugar

vanilla ice cream, to serve

Method

Put the raisins in a bowl with the brandy and leave to soften for an hour or two. In a small saucepan, warm (but don't boil) the milk and cream and add the split vanilla pod. Leave to stand for 30 minutes.

Preheat the oven to 180°C/350°F/Gas Mark 4. Butter a shallow ovenproof dish. Butter the panettone slices, cut them diagonally in half and lay in an overlapping pattern in the dish. Remove the softened raisins from the brandy, reserving the brandy, and sprinkle them over the panettone.

In a large bowl whisk the eggs with the sugar. Remove the vanilla pod from the milk and discard and add the cream and milk to the egg mixture. Add the reserved brandy and whisk. Pour this mixture over the panettone and press the slices down so that they soak in the custard. Make sure that the edges don't stick out too far above the surface of the custard.

Transfer to the preheated oven and bake for 30–40 minutes until the custard has dried and set golden brown, but before the panettone burns. Serve hot, with vanilla ice cream.

RICH ITALIAN CHOCOLATE CAKE

Method

Preheat the oven to 180°C/350°F/Gas Mark 4. Grease a 25-cm/10-inch round springform cake tin with butter and sprinkle with flour. Shake the flour around the whole of the inside of the tin so that all the butter is covered, then knock out the excess flour.

Place the hazelnuts on a baking tray and bake in the preheated oven for 5 minutes, then leave to cool. While the nuts are baking, chop the chocolate into small pieces and place in a food processor with the almonds. Pulse on and off until the mixture is the consistency of breadcrumbs.

Transfer the mixture to a large metal bowl and stir in the brandy, coffee, cinnamon, milk and half the caster sugar. Add the egg yolks, one at a time, and continue to mix, blending well. Place the roasted hazelnuts in a clean tea towel and rub vigorously to remove the skins.

Add the hazelnuts to the food processor.

Pulse on and off, until the nuts are slightly coarser than the almonds and chocolate. Add to the cake mixture and combine well.

In a clean bowl, whisk the egg whites until stiff, add the remaining caster sugar and continue to whisk until shiny. Fold the egg whites into the cake mixture with a large metal spoon, a few spoonfuls at a time, with a cutting movement of the spoon so that you don't knock too much air out of the egg whites.

Gently spoon the mixture into the prepared cake tin and bake in the centre of the oven for an hour. The cake is ready when a skewer inserted into the centre comes out dry.

Unclip the cake, turn out onto a wire rack and leave to cool. Serve with mascarpone cheese.

Ingredients
Serves 6

butter, for greasing

flour, for dusting

225 g/8 oz hazelnuts

225 g/8 oz plain chocolate, 70 per cent cocoa solids

225 g/8 oz blanched almonds

5 tbsp brandy

2 tbsp espresso coffee

1 tsp ground cinnamon

2 tbsp milk

225 g/8 oz caster sugar

5 large eggs, separated, at room temperature

mascarpone cheese, to serve

BARCELONA

It is often said that most people in the world eat to live,
but Spaniards live to eat. And nowhere is this more evident
than in Barcelona – the Catalonian capital where the
Pyrenees meet the Mediterranean – with its thriving tapas
culture and popular restaurants. Food in the city tends to be
flavoursome and traditional, rather than trendy or making
concessions to passing fads, and expensive and simple
meals alike begin with Tomato-rubbed Bread. The best
produce and other ingredients the city has to offer are on
display at La Boqueria, the famed 19th-century market. This
vast metal and glass structure is a must-see on any visit,
and the restaurants that surround the perimeter provide an
inexpensive, authentic sampling of the city's cooking.

BABY BROAD BEANS & CHORIZO

Ingredients

Serves 4

1 tbsp olive oil

250 g/9 oz fresh chorizo sausage, chopped into finger-thick slices.

4 spring onions, sliced

3 garlic cloves, crushed

100 ml/3½ fl oz chicken stock or vegetable stock, warmed

2 kg/4 lb 8 oz young broad beans in their pods, or about 750 g/1 lb 10 oz podded frozen baby broad beans

1 large handful fresh mint, chopped

salt and pepper

toasted sourdough bread, to serve

Method

Place a heavy-based frying pan over a medium heat and add the olive oil. When it's shimmering hot, add the chorizo and brown it on all sides for about 15 minutes. Remove it from the pan and set aside. Reduce the heat, add the spring onions and garlic and fry for a further 5 minutes. Add the stock and broad beans and simmer for about 3–5 minutes until the beans are just tender. Add the mint and the cooked chorizo, stir through and season with salt and pepper. Serve, with the juices, on small warmed plates, with some sourdough toast on the side.

TOMATO-RUBBED BREAD

Method

If the bread is soft, toast it under a preheated grill until lightly golden on both sides. Rub each slice of bread with half a fresh juicy tomato. If using, sprinkle over the chopped garlic and drizzle the olive oil over the top.

Ingredients

Serves 4 as part of a tapas meal

4 *slices French bread*

2 *ripe tomatoes, halved*

1 *garlic clove, finely chopped (optional)*

2 *tbsp Spanish olive oil (optional)*

GAZPACHO

Ingredients

Serves 4

1 red pepper, cored, deseeded and chopped

1 kg/2 lb 4 oz ripe tomatoes, cored and chopped

2 tbsp very finely chopped onion

3 garlic cloves, crushed

1 cucumber, peeled and chopped

100 g/3½ oz stale bread, crumbled

3 tbsp red wine vinegar or sherry vinegar

3½ tbsp olive oil, plus extra for drizzling

200 g/7 oz ice cubes (optional)

salt and pepper

Method

Set aside a handful of the red pepper, a handful of the tomatoes and half the chopped onion in the refrigerator. Put the rest in a food processor with the garlic, cucumber and the remaining onion and purée until smooth. Add the bread, vinegar and oil and whizz again. Season to taste with salt and pepper. If the soup is too thick, add the ice, then place in the refrigerator for 2 hours.

When ready to serve, check the vinegar and seasoning and ladle into bowls. Scatter over the reserved red pepper, tomatoes and onions, then drizzle over a swirl of olive oil. Serve.

FIDEUÀ

Method

To make the sofregit, put the onion and oil in a 25-cm/10-inch paella pan or heavy-based frying pan with a tight-fitting lid and place over a medium heat. Cook, stirring occasionally, for 10 minutes, or until the onions are soft and just starting to colour. Reduce the heat to very low and continue cooking for a further 10–20 minutes until they are golden brown. Add the tomatoes and their juices and the chilli, increase the heat and continue to simmer, stirring, for 15 minutes, or until the tomatoes are reduced to a pulp and start to give off the oil they have absorbed.

Meanwhile, put the stock in a saucepan with the reserved prawn shells and simmer over a low heat for 10 minutes. Strain, discard the shells, then return the liquid to the pan with the saffron and ½ teaspoon salt and bring to the boil. Turn off the heat, cover the pan and set aside.

Wipe out the sofregit pan. Add the oil to the pan and heat over a medium heat. Add the noodles and fry for 10 minutes, stirring constantly, until they are golden brown and look 'cooked'. Stir the sofregit into the noodles, then add the stock and bring to the boil, stirring with a long-handled wooden spoon: the mixture will spatter when the sofregit is added. Reduce the heat to medium and stir for 8–10 minutes until all the liquid is absorbed and the noodles are tender. Adjust the seasoning to taste.

Discard any open mussels and clams that do not close when tapped. Arrange the prawns, mussels, clams and squid on top of the noodles, reduce the heat to very low, cover the pan tightly and leave to steam for 5 minutes, or until the prawns are pink, the mussels and clams are open and the squid turn white and lose their translucency.

Discard any closed mussels or clams. Adjust the seasoning to taste. Serve immediately with lemon wedges for squeezing over each portion and a bowl of aïoli on the side.

Ingredients

Serves 4–6

700 ml/1¼ pints fish stock

12 raw king prawns, peeled, heads removed, tails left on, shells reserved

large pinch saffron threads

2 tbsp olive oil

500 g/1 lb 2 oz thin, hollow Spanish noodles (fidos, or fideu in Catalan), or angel hair pasta, broken into small pieces

12 large mussels, scrubbed and debearded

12 clams, scrubbed

6 small cleaned squid bodies with tentacles

salt and pepper

lemon wedges and aïoli, to serve

SOFREGIT

1 onion, chopped

3½ tbsp garlic-flavoured olive oil

2 large tomatoes, grated, skins and cores discarded

1 fresh red chilli, deseeded and thinly sliced

TRADITIONAL CATALAN SALT COD SALAD

Method

Place the dried salt cod in a large bowl, cover with cold water and leave to soak for at least 48 hours, changing the water occasionally.

Pat the salt cod very dry with kitchen paper and remove the skin and bones, then use your fingers to tear into fine shreds. Put in a large, non-metallic bowl with the spring onions, oil, vinegar and lemon juice and toss together. Season with freshly ground black pepper, cover and put in the refrigerator to marinate for 3 hours.

Stir in the peppers and olives. Taste and adjust the seasoning, if necessary, remembering that the cod and olives might be salty. Arrange the tomato slices on a large platter or individual plates and spoon the salad on top. Sprinkle with parsley and serve.

Ingredients

Serves 4–6

400 g/14 oz dried salt cod in one piece

6 spring onions, thinly sliced on the diagonal

6 tbsp extra virgin olive oil

1 tbsp sherry vinegar

1 tbsp lemon juice

2 large red peppers, grilled, peeled, deseeded and very finely diced

12 large black olives, stoned and sliced

2 large, juicy tomatoes, thinly sliced, to serve

2 tbsp very finely chopped fresh parsley, to garnish

pepper

CHICKEN AND HAM CROQUETTES

Ingredients

Serves 4

4 tbsp Spanish olive oil or butter

4 tbsp plain flour

200 ml/7 fl oz milk

115 g/4 oz cooked chicken, minced

55 g/2 oz Serrano or cooked ham, very finely chopped

1 tbsp chopped fresh flat-leaf parsley

small pinch of freshly grated nutmeg

1 egg, beaten

55 g/2 oz day-old white breadcrumbs

sunflower oil, for deep-frying

salt and pepper

Method

Heat the olive oil or butter in a saucepan. Stir in the flour to form a paste and cook gently for 1 minute, stirring constantly. Remove the saucepan from the heat and gradually stir in the milk until smooth. Return to the heat and slowly bring to the boil, stirring constantly, until the mixture boils and begins to thicken.

Remove the saucepan from the heat, add the minced chicken and beat until the mixture is smooth. Add the chopped ham, parsley and nutmeg and mix well. Season the mixture to taste with salt and pepper. Spread the chicken mixture in a dish and leave for 30 minutes until cool, then cover and leave to chill for 2–3 hours or overnight.

When the chicken mixture has chilled, pour the beaten egg onto a plate and spread the breadcrumbs out on a separate plate. Divide the chicken mixture into 8 equal-sized portions. With dampened hands, form each portion into a cylindrical shape. Dip the croquettes, one at a time, in the beaten egg, then roll in the breadcrumbs to coat them. Place on a plate and chill for 1 hour.

To cook, heat the sunflower oil in a deep-fat fryer to 180–190°C/350–375°F, or until a cube of bread browns in 30 seconds. Add the croquettes, in batches to prevent the temperature of the oil from dropping, and deep-fry for 5–10 minutes, or until golden brown and crispy. Remove with a slotted spoon and drain well on kitchen paper. Serve the chicken and ham croquettes piping hot.

CATALAN PORK STEW

Ingredients

Serves 4–6

olive oil, for browning

2 kg/4 lb 8 oz boneless pork shoulder, cut into 7.5-cm/3-in chunks and patted dry

bouquet garni of parsley, thyme and a bay leaf, tied with string

750 ml/1⅓ pints white Catalan wine, such as Chenin Blanc

3–4 carrots, peeled and cut into 1-cm/½-inch slices

800 g/1 lb 2 oz canned chickpeas, drained and rinsed

salt and pepper

SOFREGIT

2 onions, chopped

125 ml/4 fl oz olive oil

4 large tomatoes, grated, skins and cores discarded

4 large garlic cloves, finely chopped

1 tbsp hot Spanish paprika

PICADA

1 slice day-old country bread, about 30 g/1 oz, fried in olive oil

1 tbsp blanched almonds, toasted

1 tbsp skinned hazelnuts, toasted

2 garlic cloves, crushed

30 g/1 oz dark Spanish chocolate

olive oil, as required

Method

To make the sofregit, put the onions and oil in a large flameproof casserole and place over a medium–high heat. Cook, stirring occasionally, for 10 minutes. Reduce the heat to very low and continue cooking for a further 10–20 minutes, until the onions are golden brown. Add the tomatoes and their juices, the garlic and the paprika, increase the heat and continue to simmer, stirring, for 15 minutes, or until the tomatoes are reduced to a pulp and start to give off the oil they have absorbed.

Preheat the oven to 160°C/325°F/Gas Mark 3. Remove the sofregit and set aside. Wipe out the casserole, add a thin layer of oil and heat over a medium–high heat. Brown the pork on all sides in batches, adding more oil if necessary. Pour off any excess fat. Return the pork to the casserole. Stir in the sofregit, herbs, and salt and pepper to taste. Pour in the wine and enough water to cover all the meat, then bring to the boil. Cover and place in the preheated oven. After 1¼ hours stir in the carrots, re-cover the casserole and return to the oven for 30 minutes, or until the pork and carrots are tender.

Meanwhile, to make the picada, tear the bread into a food processor, then add the almonds, hazelnuts, garlic and chocolate and whizz until finely blended. With the motor running, slowly pour in enough olive oil to form a thick paste.

Transfer the casserole to the hob. Remove the pork and carrots and set aside. Bring the cooking liquid to the boil and place several ladlefuls in a heatproof bowl. Stir in the picada until well blended, then stir this mixture into the cooking liquid and continue boiling for 2 minutes. Reduce the heat and add the pork, carrots and chickpeas. Simmer for about 5 minutes, or until the stew thickens and the chickpeas are hot. Adjust the seasoning, if necessary, and serve.

FLAN

Ingredients

Makes 5

500 ml/18 fl oz milk

½ orange with 2 long, thin pieces of rind removed and reserved

1 vanilla pod, split, or ½ tsp vanilla extract

175 g/6 oz caster sugar

butter, for greasing the dish

3 large eggs, plus 2 large egg yolks

Method

Pour the milk into a saucepan with the orange rind and vanilla pod. Bring to the boil, then remove from the heat and stir in 100 g/3½ oz of the sugar; set aside for at least 30 minutes to infuse.

Meanwhile, put the remaining sugar and 4 tablespoons of water in another saucepan over a medium–high heat. Stir until the sugar dissolves, then boil without stirring until the caramel turns deep golden brown.

Immediately remove the saucepan from the heat and squeeze in a few drops of orange juice to stop the cooking. Pour into a lightly buttered 1.2-litre/2-pint soufflé dish and swirl to cover the base; set aside.

When the milk has infused, return the saucepan to the heat and bring the milk to a simmer. Beat the whole eggs and egg yolks together in a heatproof bowl. Pour the warm milk into the eggs, whisking constantly. Strain this mixture into the soufflé dish.

Place the soufflé dish in a roasting tin and pour in enough boiling water to come halfway up the sides of the dish. Bake in a preheated oven, 160°C/325°F/Gas Mark 3, for 75–90 minutes until set and a knife inserted in the centre comes out clean.

Remove the soufflé dish from the roasting tin and set aside to cool completely. Cover and chill overnight.

To serve, run a metal spatula around the side of the dish, then invert onto a serving plate with a rim, shaking firmly to release.

CHOCOLATE HAZELNUT CAKE

Method

Put 55 g/2 oz of the hazelnuts in a blender and blitz until very finely ground, then set aside. Preheat the oven to 180°C/350°F/ Gas Mark 4 and line the base of a 23-cm/ 9-inch round cake tin with baking paper.

Put the butter and chocolate in a heatproof bowl set over a saucepan of gently simmering water and heat until melted. Set aside to cool. Beat the eggs, sugar and vanilla extract together for 3 minutes, until light and fluffy. Stir in the chocolate and butter. Sift over the flour, baking powder, salt and ground hazelnuts, rubbing the hazelnuts through the sieve with a wooden spoon. Toss the raisins and whole hazelnuts with the 1 tablespoon of flour, then fold into the mixture.

Pour the mixture into the prepared tin and smooth the surface. Bake for 45 minutes, or until a cocktail stick inserted in the centre comes out clean and the cake comes away from the side of the tin. Leave to cool in the tin for 10 minutes, turn out, remove the paper and leave to cool on a wire rack. Transfer to a plate and sift over some icing sugar.

Ingredients

Serves 6

125g/4½ oz skinned hazelnuts, lightly toasted

175 g/6 oz butter, softened, plus extra for greasing

85 g/3 oz dark Spanish chocolate
　　　(at least 85% cocoa solids)

4 large eggs, beaten

100 g/3½ oz sugar

1 tsp vanilla extract

55 g/2 oz plain flour, plus 1 tbsp extra

½ tsp baking powder

pinch of salt

140 g/5 oz raisins, soaked in 2 tbsp
　　　Spanish brandy

icing sugar, to decorate

GOAT'S CHEESE WITH HONEY & WALNUTS

Ingredients

Serves 4

about 175 g/6 oz goat's cheese, such as Monte Enebro, in one piece

about 115 g/4 oz clear honey, such as orange-blossom or thyme-flavoured

100 g/3½ oz walnut halves, chopped

Method

Remove the cheese from the fridge at least 20 minutes before serving to allow it to come to room temperature.

Pour the honey into a bowl. Place the walnuts in another bowl.

Serve the cheese on a board with a cheese knife and let everyone cut a slice for themselves, drizzling over some honey, with a dipper, if available, and sprinkling with chopped walnuts.

Alternatively, cut the cheese into four quarters and place a slice on each of four serving plates. Drizzle over some honey, sprinkle with chopped nuts and serve.

BERLIN

Meat reigns supreme in Berlin, but there is more to the city's food culture than just sausages, sauerkraut and beer. Meals are filling and traditional. Pork, potatoes and apples feature in many hearty, savoury dishes, yet pastry chefs also make their mark with traditional Stollen, a Christmas favourite, and Poppy Seed Cake, often enjoyed with a cup of strong coffee. The meat-and-fruit combination is especially popular in classics such as Fried Calf's Liver with Apples & Onions, a filling meal easily complemented by one of the local beers. For many Berliners a meal simply isn't complete without potatoes in one form or another – Berlin Meatballs with Potato Salad and Potato Soup are popular examples.

BERLIN MEATBALLS & POTATO SALAD

Ingredients

Serves 3–4

2 thick slices day-old white bread, crusts removed

250 ml/9 fl oz warm milk

250 g/9 oz lean minced beef

250 g/9 oz lean minced pork

1 large egg, lightly beaten

1 tbsp chopped fresh parsley

salt and freshly ground white pepper

freshly grated nutmeg

curry powder

55 g/2 oz butter

1 large onion, sliced thinly into rings

salt and pepper

salad

750 g/1 lb 10 oz waxy new potatoes, scraped

2–3 tbsp hot veal or beef stock

1 tbsp vinegar

85 g/3 oz sweet onion, chopped

2 tbsp white wine vinegar

1 tsp butter

4 tbsp diced bacon

1 tsp cornflour

1 tsp brown sugar

2 tbsp water

2 tbsp soured cream

1 tbsp fresh chives, finely chopped

1 tbsp fresh parsley, finely chopped

Method

Place the bread in a bowl, pour over the milk and let soak for 10 minutes. Place the minced beef and pork in a bowl and mix together well. Squeeze any excess milk out of the bread and add the bread to the meat in the bowl. Add the beaten egg and the parsley, then add salt and pepper, nutmeg and curry powder to taste. Shape the meat mixture into balls and flatten them slightly. Heat the butter in a heavy-based frying pan over a medium–high and fry the meatballs, turning once, for 5–7 minutes, or until browned all over and cooked through. Transfer to a warmed serving dish. Add the onion rings to the pan and fry until crisp and lightly browned.

To make the salad, steam the new potatoes, for 15–20 minutes, until tender. Slice the cooked potatoes into a warm dish, gently stir in enough hot stock to coat, and set aside to keep warm. Mix the onion and vinegar together. Melt the butter in a small pan over a medium heat and cook the bacon for 2 minutes. Mix together the cornflour, sugar and water and add to the pan with the onion and vinegar mixture. Cook, stirring, for 2–3 minutes, until the mixture clears and thickens. Remove from the heat and stir in the soured cream and herbs. Season to taste with salt and pepper.

Serve the potato salad with the meatballs and onion rings piled on top.

POTATO SOUP

Ingredients

Serves 4

3 tbsp butter

1 medium onion, peeled and chopped

1 leek, tough outer leaves removed, sliced

1 large carrot, peeled and chopped

1 small parsnip, peeled and chopped

1 small celeriac, peeled and chopped

1 celery stalk, chopped

1 Hamburg parsley root, peeled and finely diced

1 sprig of fresh parsley

450 g/1 lb floury potatoes, cut into chunks

3 tbsp flour

1.2 litres/2 pints water

2 tsp dried marjoram

salt and pepper

2 tbsp each finely chopped fresh parsley and dill, to garnish

Method

Melt the butter in a large, heavy-based saucepan, add the onion, leek, carrot, parsnip, celeriac, celery stalk, parsley root and parsley sprig and cook over medium heat, stirring constantly, for 7–8 minutes, or until the vegetables are soft and golden.

Add the potatoes and cook, stirring, for a further 4–5 minutes, or until the potatoes start to colour. Stir in the flour and cook until it starts to brown.

Pour over the water, stir in the marjoram, season to taste with salt and pepper and bring to the boil. Reduce the heat and simmer for 30 minutes, or until the potatoes are tender.

Transfer the soup to a food processor and process until smooth. Return to the pan and heat through, then serve garnished with chopped parsley and dill.

POTATO FRITTERS

Ingredients

Serves 4–5

1 kg/2 lb 4 oz floury potatoes, peeled

1 large egg

2 tbsp flour

vegetable oil, for frying

salt

apple sauce, to serve

Method

Coarsely grate the potatoes into a bowl of water to prevent discoloration, then drain them and dry thoroughly on a clean tea towel. Transfer to a bowl, then add the egg, salt to taste and flour, and mix thoroughly.

Pour vegetable oil into a large, heavy-based frying pan to a depth of 1 cm/½ inch and place over a medium–high heat. When the oil is hot, drop in large spoonfuls of the potato mixture, in batches of 3 or 4, set well apart. Flatten each fritter with a palette knife and fry, turning once, until golden brown on both sides. Remove from the pan and drain on kitchen paper, then keep warm while you cook the remaining fritters. Serve warm with apple sauce.

FRIED CALF'S LIVER WITH APPLES & ONIONS

Method

Melt 15 g/½ oz of the butter in a frying pan over a medium–low heat and fry the apple slices on both sides until just soft. Carefully remove from the pan with a fish slice and keep warm.

Add the onion slices to the pan and fry until golden, adding a little more butter if necessary.

Meanwhile, melt the remaining butter over low heat in another frying pan. Dust the liver slices Lightly dust the liver slices with flour and fry very gently for about 4 minutes, turning frequently, until golden brown all over on the outside but still pink inside.

Remove from the heat and season with salt, white pepper and nutmeg to taste. Serve with the apple and onion slices on top, accompanied by red cabbage and mashed potato.

Ingredients

Serves 4

about 55 g/2 oz butter

2 green dessert apples, peeled, cored and sliced

2 medium onions, peeled and sliced into rings

450 g/1 lb calf's liver, cut into 5 mm/¼-inch slices

1 tbsp flour

salt and freshly ground white pepper

freshly grated nutmeg

red cabbage and mashed potato, to serve

MEATBALLS IN LEMON-CAPER SAUCE

Method

Place the bread in a small bowl, cover with the water and soak for 10 minutes, then squeeze out any excess water. Place the soaked bread in a large mixing bowl and add the minced beef and veal, marjoram, egg yolks and salt and pepper to taste.

Melt the butter in a saucepan and fry the onion until lightly coloured. Add it to the meat mixture with the lemon rind and anchovies and mix well. Form the mixture into small balls.

Bring the stock to the boil in a large, heavy-based saucepan, add the meatballs, then reduce the heat to medium–low and simmer for about 20 minutes, or until the meatballs rise to the surface. Remove with a slotted spoon and keep warm. Reserve the stock.

To make the sauce, melt the butter in a large saucepan over a medium heat. Whisk in the flour and cook for 1 minute, still whisking, then gradually whisk in the reserved stock. Add the capers and lemon juice and season to taste. Add the meatballs and heat through for 5 minutes. Mix the egg yolks into the soured cream and stir into the meatballs and sauce. Heat very gently to thicken the sauce, then serve the meatballs on a bed of egg noodles, sprinkled with extra freshly ground black pepper.

Ingredients

Serves 4

2 thick slices day-old white bread, crusts removed

250 ml/9 fl oz cold water

250 g/9 oz lean minced beef

250 g/9 oz lean minced veal or pork

1½ tsp chopped fresh marjoram or ½ tsp dried marjoram

2 medium egg yolks

1 tbsp butter

1 medium onion, grated

finely grated rind of ½ lemon

3 anchovy fillets, finely chopped

750 ml/1⅓ chicken stock

salt and pepper

freshly cooked egg noodles, to serve

sauce

2 tbsp butter

2 tbsp flour

2 tbsp capers, chopped

1 tbsp lemon juice

2 medium egg yolks

150 ml/5 fl oz soured cream

PORK HOCKS WITH SAUERKRAUT

Ingredients

Serves 6

6 pork hocks, cleaned, split and rinsed under cold running water

1 onion, peeled and left whole

2 bay leaves

1 tbsp pickling spice

8 black peppercorns, lightly crushed

salt

sauerkraut, to serve

fresh parsley, finely chopped, to garnish

Method

Place the pork hocks in a large, heavy-based saucepan and pour over water to cover. Add the onion, bay leaves, pickling spice and peppercorns and season to taste with salt. Cover the pan, bring to the boil, reduce the heat and simmer over a medium–low heat for about 3 hours, or until the meat is tender but still clinging to the bone. Remove the hocks from the pan and drain well.

Divide the pork hocks between individual plates and serve with sauerkraut, garnished with fresh parsley.

SAUERBRAUTEN WITH RED CABBAGE

Ingredients

Serves 8

1.8 kg/4 lb boneless beef joint, such as silverside

2 tbsp lard or vegetable oil

1 onion, chopped

250 g/9 oz carrots, chopped

2 celery sticks, chopped

2 tbsp plain flour

100 ml/3½ fl oz water

100 g/3½ oz ginger biscuits, crumbled

boiled potatoes and red cabbage, to serve

salt and pepper

marinade

375 ml/13 fl oz red wine

275 ml/9½ fl oz red wine vinegar

225 ml/8 fl oz water

2 onions, quartered

2 tsp black peppercorns, slightly crushed

2 tsp juniper berries, slightly crushed

4 bay leaves

2 cloves

1 tbsp salt

2 tbsp sugar

Method

Place all the marinade ingredients in a non-metallic bowl large enough to hold the meat and stir until the sugar and salt dissolve. Add the meat, cover and place in a cool place for 3 days. Turn the meat in the marinade each morning and evening.

Preheat the oven to 160°C/325°F/Gas Mark 3. Remove the meat from the marinade and pat dry with kitchen paper. Season with salt and pepper. Strain the marinade and discard the spices and onions. Place a large flameproof casserole over a high heat and add the lard. When hot, add the beef and brown it quickly on all sides. Remove it and reserve. Reduce the heat a little, add the vegetables and fry for 5 minutes. Add the flour, stir and cook for a further 2 minutes. Add 500 ml/18 fl oz of the marinade and the water.

Cover the casserole tightly, place in the preheated oven and cook for 2½ hours, checking after 1½ hours to make sure it isn't drying out. If it is, add more marinade.

Remove the meat from the casserole, cover and keep warm while you make the sauce. Strain the remaining cooking liquid from the casserole into a saucepan and add enough marinade to make it up to about 500 ml/18 fl oz. Add the crumbled biscuits and simmer for 15 minutes until it thickens. Season to taste.

Carve the meat and serve with the sauce, boiled potatoes and red cabbage.

POPPY SEED CAKE

Ingredients

Serves 4

pastry

140 g/5 oz butter, at room temperature

generous 3 tbsp caster sugar

pinch of salt

1 large egg

200 g/7 oz flour

filling

140 g/5 oz ground poppy seeds

6 tbsp milk

115 g/4 oz granulated sugar

55 g/2 oz grated plain chocolate

55 g/2 oz raisins

55 g/2 oz candied peel, chopped

55 g/2 oz blanched almonds, grated

1 large egg, beaten

1 tbsp caster sugar

1 tbsp whole poppy seeds

Method

To make the pastry, beat together the butter, sugar and salt, add the egg, then stir in the flour and just enough cold water to make a soft dough. Cover in clingfilm and chill in the refrigerator for 1 hour.

Meanwhile, to make the filling, place the poppy seeds and milk in a saucepan and simmer, stirring, for 2 minutes. Remove the pan from the heat and stir in the granulated sugar, chocolate, raisins, candied peel and almonds. Set aside 1 teaspoon of the beaten egg and beat the remainder into the mixture.

Roll the pastry out thinly on a lightly floured counter and cut 4 x 20-cm/8-inch circles. Place one circle in a 20-cm/8-inch loose-bottom tart pan and spread over one-third of the filling. Repeat the layers, finishing with the last pastry circle. Press the edges together very lightly, then make a hole in the centre with the handle of a wooden spoon.

Brush the cake with the reserved beaten egg, then sprinkle with the caster sugar and whole poppy seeds. Bake in a preheated oven, 160°C/325°F/ Gas Mark 3, for about 45 minutes, until golden. Serve warm or cold.

BAKED APPLES with VANILLA SAUCE

Ingredients

Serves 4

4 large cooking apples, washed and dried

55 g/2 oz marzipan

about 1 tbsp rum

2 tbsp sultanas

2 tbsp butter

300 ml/10 fl oz dry white wine

4 tbsp apricot jam

vanilla sauce

450 ml/16 fl oz milk

½ vanilla pod

3 egg yolks

55 g/2 oz sugar

2 tsp cornflour

Method

Core the apples most of the way through from the stalk end, then score lightly around the middle with a sharp knife. Using a fork, soften the marzipan with the rum, then work in the sultanas. Place a little butter in each apple, then divide the marzipan filling between them and top with a little more butter.

Preheat the oven to 190°C/375°F/Gas Mark 5. Place the apples in a baking dish and pour in the wine. Bake for 25–30 minutes, basting occasionally with the wine. Transfer to a serving dish. Strain the wine into a saucepan, stir in the apricot jam and simmer, stirring, until reduced to a thick syrup. Spoon over the apples and cool for 1 hour.

To make the vanilla sauce, bring the milk and vanilla to scalding point in a heatproof bowl set over a saucepan of simmering water. Beat the egg yolks, sugar and cornflour in a large, heatproof bowl until light and frothy. Gradually add the milk, stirring constantly. Set over the pan of simmering water and cook, stirring, until the sauce thickens. Remove the vanilla pod and serve the sauce with the apples.

STOLLEN

Ingredients

Serves 8

150 ml/5 fl oz lukewarm milk

55 g/2 oz caster sugar

2 tsp active dried yeast

350 g/12 oz strong white bread flour

½ tsp salt

115 g/4 oz butter, softened, plus extra for greasing

1 medium egg, beaten

40 g/1½ oz currants

55 g/2 oz sultanas

55 g/2 oz candied peel, finely diced

55 g/2 oz glacé cherries

25 g/1 oz blanched almonds, chopped

grated rind of ½ lemon

175 g/6 oz marzipan, formed into a 23-cm/ 9-inch sausage

115 g/4 oz icing sugar, sifted

1 tbsp water

Method

Pour the warm milk into a small bowl, add 1 teaspoon of the sugar, sprinkle over the yeast, and whisk thoroughly. Set aside for 10 minutes, until a frothy head has formed.

Set aside 2 tablespoons of flour and sift the rest into a large mixing bowl with the salt and remaining sugar. Make a well in the centre, pour in the yeast mixture, then add the butter and beaten egg. Mix well to form a soft dough.

Work in the currants, sultanas, peel, cherries, almonds and lemon rind, then transfer the dough to a counter and knead for 5 minutes, until smooth and elastic. Place in a clean bowl, cover with clingfilm and stand in a warm place for 1½–2 hours, until doubled in size.

Sprinkle the reserved flour onto a counter and turn out the dough onto it. Punch out the air, then knead again until smooth and elastic. Roll out to a 25 x 20-cm/10 x 8-inch rectangle and place the marzipan in the centre.

Fold the dough over the marzipan and place, seam-side down, on a greased baking sheet. Cover and set aside until doubled in size, then bake in a preheated oven, 190°C/ 375°F/Gas Mark 5, for 35–40 minutes, until risen and golden. Transfer to a wire rack to cool a little.

Mix the icing sugar with the water and spread it thinly over the stollen while it is still warm. Cut into slices and serve.

ΠEW DELHI

Food in Delhi is as exciting and varied as India's capital city itself. Spiced street food and snacks, or chaats, are an integral part of city life, sometimes eaten outdoors on the go or as part of an indoor meal. While luxury hotels serve refined international cuisine for the wealthy and tourists, it is the everyday food from the thousands of stalls in markets, bazaars and on street corners that capture the spirit of India, with its dynamic mix of religions that so strongly influence the eating habits of millions. Lamb Burras, Whole Tandoori Chickens and Salt Lassis are just some of the recipes that make it easy to savour an authentic flavour of India at home. With a large resident vegetarian population, visiting vegetarians have more choices here than in many other cities, with restaurants always offering 'non-meat' options.

TARKA DHAL

Ingredients

Serves 4

200 g/7 oz red split lentils

850 ml/1½ pints water

1 tsp salt, or to taste

2 tsp sunflower or olive oil

½ tsp black or brown mustard seeds

½ tsp cumin seeds

4 shallots, finely chopped

2 green chillies, chopped
(deseeded if you like)

1 tsp ground turmeric

1 tsp ground cumin

1 fresh tomato, chopped

2 tbsp chopped fresh coriander leaves

basmati rice or naan, to serve

Method

Wash the lentils until the water runs clear and put into a medium-sized saucepan. Add the water and bring to the boil. Reduce the heat to medium and skim off the froth. Cook, uncovered, for 10 minutes. Reduce the heat to low, cover and cook for 45 minutes, stirring occasionally to ensure that the lentils do not stick to the bottom of the pan as they thicken. Stir in the salt.

Meanwhile, heat the oil in a small saucepan over a medium heat. When hot but not smoking, add the mustard seeds, followed by the cumin seeds. Add the shallots and chillies and cook, stirring, for 2–3 minutes, then add the turmeric and ground cumin. Add the tomato and cook, stirring, for 30 seconds.

Fold the shallot mixture into the cooked lentils. Stir in the coriander, remove from the heat and serve immediately with basmati rice.

ALOO TIKA

Ingredients

Serves 4

2 large baking potatoes, about 225 g/8 oz each

125 g/4½ oz frozen peas

1 tsp garam masala

1 tsp salt

½ tsp turmeric

½ red onion, very finely chopped

½ fresh red chilli, deseeded and very finely chopped

sunflower oil or groundnut oil, for oiling and frying

55 g/2 oz chickpea flour, seasoned with salt and pepper

pepper

selection of chutneys, relishes and dips, to serve

Method

Put the potatoes in a large saucepan of water, bring to the boil and cook for 15 minutes, or until just tender. Do not overcook. Drain the potatoes and set aside until cool enough to handle, then peel and grate them into a large bowl.

Bring a saucepan of lightly salted water to the boil, add the peas and cook for 5 minutes, or until tender. Drain well and add to the bowl with the potatoes. Add the garam masala, salt, turmeric, and pepper to taste and use your hands to mix. Add the onion and chilli and use your hands to work everything together.

Wash and dry your hands, then lightly grease them with the oil. Roll the potato mixture into 16 equal balls, then flatten them between your palms. Put the chickpea flour on a plate. Pat the flour onto both sides of the patties, shaking off the excess.

Heat about 1 cm/½ inch of the oil in a large frying pan over a high heat. Fry the pattie in batches for 2 minutes on each side, or until golden brown and crisp.

Serve warm, with a selection of chutneys, relishes and dips.

SAVOURY CHEESECAKES

Ingredients

Makes 8

2 large slices day- or two-day-old white bread, crusts removed

225 g/8 oz paneer, halloumi cheese or firm tofu (drained weight), grated

3 shallots, finely chopped

1 tsp fennel seeds

½ tsp cumin seeds

1 tbsp chopped fresh mint leaves or ½ tsp dried mint

2 tbsp chopped fresh coriander leaves

1 tsp ginger purée

25g/1 oz flaked almonds, lightly crushed (optional)

1 green chilli, chopped (deseeded if you like)

½ tsp garam masala

½ tsp chilli powder (optional)

½ tsp salt, or to taste

1 tbsp lemon juice

1 large egg, beaten

sunflower or vegetable oil, for shallow-frying

Method

Soak the bread slices in a bowl of water for 1–2 minutes, then squeeze out all the water and crumble the slices between your palms. Put the bread in a large bowl and add all the remaining ingredients, except the oil. Mix well to form a binding consistency.

Divide the mixture in half and shape each half into 4 equal-sized, flat cakes 5 mm/¼ inch thick.

Pour oil into a frying pan to a depth of 2.5 cm/ 1 inch and heat over a medium heat. Add the cakes and cook for 5 minutes on each side, or until well browned. Drain on kitchen paper and serve hot.

WHOLE TANDOORI CHICKEN

Method

Cut two slits into each chicken leg and two into each thigh. They should just reach the bone. Make two shallower cuts into the fleshiest part of each breast. These are to allow the marinade to penetrate into the meat.

Mix all of the remaining ingredients together in a food processor and blend to a smooth paste. Place the chicken in a large, non-metallic dish and cover it in the paste, massaging it deep into the skin and flesh. Place the chicken, uncovered, in the refrigerator to marinate for as long as possible – preferably 24 hours.

Remove the chicken from the refrigerator an hour before cooking to warm it to room temperature. Preheat the oven to 220°C/425°F/Gas Mark 7. Place the chicken in the oven and cook, uncovered, for 20 minutes, then reduce the heat to 180°C/350°F/Gas Mark 4. Baste the chicken and cook for another 35 minutes. Turn off the oven and open the door, leaving the chicken inside to rest for 20 minutes. Serve with rice, lime wedges and hot lime pickle.

Ingredients

Serves 4

1 chicken, 1.5 kg/3 lb 5 oz

2 tsp garam masala spice mix

300 ml/10 fl oz natural yogurt

1 onion, finely chopped

2 garlic cloves, crushed

2.5-cm/1-inch piece of fresh ginger, peeled and grated

juice of 1 lemon

2 tbsp tomato purée

1 tsp chilli powder

1 tsp ground cumin

1 tsp turmeric

1 tbsp paprika (not smoked)

1 tsp salt

to serve

basmati rice, naan bread or slipper bread

lime wedges

hot lime pickle

BUTTER CHICKEN

Method

Put the onion and garlic and ginger paste in a food processor, blender or spice grinder and whizz together until a paste forms. Add the tomatoes, chilli powder, sugar and a pinch of salt and whizz again until blended.

Melt the ghee in a wok or large frying pan over a medium–high heat. Add the tomato mixture and water and stir in the tomato pureé.

Bring the mixture to the boil, stirring, then reduce the heat to very low and simmer for 5 minutes, stirring occasionally, until the sauce thickens.

Stir in half the butter, the garam masala, cumin and coriander. Add the chicken pieces and stir around until they are well coated. Simmer for a further 10 minutes, or until the chicken is hot. Taste and adjust the seasoning, if necessary.

Lightly beat the cream in a small bowl and stir in several tablespoons of the hot sauce, beating constantly. Stir the cream mixture into the tomato sauce, then add the remaining butter and stir until it melts. Garnish with chopped cashew nuts and coriander sprigs and serve straight from the pan.

Ingredients

Serves 4–6

1 onion, chopped

1½ tbsp garlic and ginger paste

400 g/14 oz canned chopped tomatoes

¼–½ tsp chilli powder

pinch of sugar

30 g/1 oz ghee or 2 tbsp vegetable or groundnut oil

125 ml/4 fl oz water

1 tbsp tomato purée

40 g/1½ oz butter, cut into small pieces

½ tsp garam masala

½ tsp ground cumin

½ tsp ground coriander

8 cooked tandoori chicken pieces

4 tbsp double cream

salt and pepper

chopped cashew nuts and fresh coriander sprigs, to garnish

MUTTON BUPPA

Ingredients
Makes 12

12 rib lamb chops, about 3.5 cm/1½ inches thick, with the meat of each chop sliced several times and the bones scraped

vegetable oil, for greasing

40 g/1½ oz ghee or butter, melted

chopped fresh coriander

tandoori marinade

300 g/10½ oz natural yogurt, strained through muslin for at least 2 hours, or 200 g/7 oz Greek-style yogurt

2 large garlic cloves, finely chopped

½ tbsp grated fresh ginger

1 tsp ground cinnamon

1 tsp ground cumin

½ tsp ground coriander

½ tsp cayenne pepper, or to taste

pinch ground cloves

pinch ground turmeric

salt and pepper

Method

To make the marinade, put all the ingredients, with some salt and pepper, into a polythene bag large enough to hold all the chops and mix together well. Add the ribs, seal the bag and leave to marinate for 4–24 hours.

When ready to cook, line a grill pan with foil and brush the rack with a little vegetable oil. Remove the chops from the marinade and wipe the ribs clean. Arrange the chops on the rack and drizzle with half the ghee.

Cook the chops for 10 minutes, then turn over and drizzle with the remaining ghee. Continue grilling for a further 8 minutes for medium or 10 minutes for well done. Leave to stand for at least 2 minutes, then sprinkle with coriander and serve. These can be served hot or cold.

MEATBALLS IN CREAMY CASHEW NUT SAUCE

Ingredients

Serves 4

450 g/1 lb fresh lean lamb mince

1 tbsp thick set natural yogurt

1 egg, beaten

½ tsp ground cardamom

½ tsp ground nutmeg

½ tsp pepper

½ tsp dried mint

½ tsp salt, or to taste

300 ml/10 fl oz water

2.5-cm/1-inch piece cinnamon stick

5 green cardamom pods

5 cloves

2 bay leaves

3 tbsp sunflower or olive oil

1 onion, finely chopped

2 tsp garlic purée

1 tsp ground ginger

1 tsp ground fennel seeds

½ tsp ground turmeric

½–1 tsp chilli powder

125 g/4½ oz raw cashew nuts, soaked in 150 ml/5 fl oz boiling water for 20 minutes

150 ml/5 fl oz double cream

1 tbsp crushed pistachio nuts, to garnish

Method

Put the lamb mince in a mixing bowl and add the yogurt, egg, cardamom, nutmeg, pepper, mint and salt. Knead the mince until it is smooth and velvety. Chill for 30–40 minutes, then divide into quarters. Make five balls out of each quarter and roll them between your palms to make them smooth and neat.

Bring the 300 ml/10 fl oz water to the boil in a large shallow pan and add all the whole spices and the bay leaves. Arrange the meatballs in a single layer in the spiced liquid, reduce the heat to medium, cover the pan and cook for 12–15 minutes. Remove the meatballs, cover and keep hot. Strain the spiced stock and set aside.

Wipe out the pan and add the oil. Place over a medium heat and add the onion and garlic purée. Cook until the mixture begins to brown and add the ground ginger, ground fennel seeds, turmeric and chilli powder. Stir-fry for 2–3 minutes, then add the strained stock and meatballs. Bring to the boil, reduce the heat to low, cover and simmer for 10–12 minutes.

Meanwhile, purée the cashews in a blender and add to the meatball mixture along with the cream. Simmer for a further 5–6 minutes, then remove from the heat. Garnish with crushed pistachio nuts and serve.

ALMOND AND PISTACHIO DESSERT

Ingredients

Serves 6

75 g/2¾ oz unsalted butter
200 g/7 oz ground almonds
200 g/7 oz sugar
150 ml/5 fl oz single cream
8 almonds, chopped
10 pistachio nuts, chopped

Method

Melt the butter in a heavy-based saucepan, preferably non-stick, stirring well. Add the ground almonds, sugar and cream, stirring well. Reduce the heat and stir constantly for 10–12 minutes, scraping the base of the saucepan.

Increase the heat until the mixture turns a little darker in colour.

Transfer the almond mixture to a large, shallow serving dish and smooth the top with the back of a spoon.

Decorate the top of the dessert with the chopped almonds and pistachio nuts. Leave to set for 1 hour, then cut into diamond shapes and serve cold.

SALT LASSI

Ingredients

Serves 4–6

700 ml/1¼ pints natural yogurt

½ tsp salt

¼ tsp sugar

250 ml/9 fl oz cold water

ice cubes

ground cumin and fresh mint sprigs,
to decorate

Method

Beat the yogurt, salt and sugar together in a jug or bowl, then add the water and whisk until frothy.

Fill 4 or 6 glasses with ice cubes and pour over the yogurt mixture. Lightly dust the top of each glass with ground cumin and decorate with mint sprigs.

AAM KI KULFI

Ingredients

Serves 6–8

375 g/13 oz canned evaporated milk

300 ml/10 fl oz single cream

25 g/1 oz ground almonds

115–140 g/4–5 oz granulated sugar

450 g/1 lb mango purée

1 tsp freshly ground cardamom seeds

25 g/1 oz shelled unsalted pistachio nuts,
to decorate

Method

Pour the evaporated milk and cream into a heavy-based saucepan and stir to mix. Put over a medium heat. Mix the ground almonds and sugar together, then add to the milk mixture. Cook, stirring, for 6–8 minutes, until the mixture thickens slightly.

Remove from the heat and leave the mixture to cool completely, stirring from time to time to prevent a skin forming. When completely cold, stir in the mango purée and ground cardamom.

Meanwhile, preheat a small saucepan over a medium heat, add the pistachio nuts and toast for 2–3 minutes. Leave to cool, then lightly crush. Store in an airtight container until required.

Kulfi is set in traditional conical-shaped plastic or steel moulds, which you can buy from Asian stores, but you can use decorative individual jelly moulds or ice lolly moulds instead. Fill the containers of your choice with the kulfi mixture and freeze for 5–6 hours. Traditional moulds hold about 2 tablespoons of the kulfi mixture, but you can use larger containers if you like. Transfer the kulfi to the refrigerator for 40 minutes. Serve sprinkled with the crushed pistachio nuts to decorate.

BANGKOK

Clear, clean flavours from coconut, ginger, lime, tamarind and blasts of heat from some of the world's hottest chillies sum up the essence of Bangkok's tantalizing food. The best Thai cooking involves complex preparation and has evolved from the royal kitchens, but Bangkok also has an established tradition of street food, prepared to order by vendors for eating on the go. Easy-to-make Green Chicken Curry, for example, is now popular around the world. All the dishes of a typical Bangkok meal are served at once. This provides an interesting mix of textures from steamed and crisp stir-fried dishes, soft noodles and tender rice and exciting flavour combinations, along with refreshing and crunchy salads, meals that satisfy several senses simultaneously.

THAI TOM YUM SOUP WITH FISH

Ingredients

serves 6

1.5 litres/2¾ pints light chicken stock

6 lemon grass stalks, crushed to release their flavour

3 tbsp very finely chopped coriander roots

10 kaffir lime leaves, central stalks torn off

1 red chilli, deseeded and finely chopped

2.5-cm/1-inch piece of galangal (or fresh ginger), peeled and thinly sliced

3 tbsp fish sauce

1 tbsp sugar

500 g/1 lb 2 oz raw prawns, shelled except for the tails

500 g/1 lb 2 oz firm white fish, such as cod or monkfish, chopped into bite-sized pieces

225 g/8 oz canned bamboo shoots or water chestnuts

12 cherry tomatoes, halved

juice of 2 limes

handful fresh coriander leaves and handful fresh basil leaves, chopped, to garnish

Method

Pour the stock into a large saucepan and add the lemon grass, coriander roots, lime leaves, chilli, galangal, fish sauce and sugar. Cover the saucepan. Bring to the boil, then reduce the heat and simmer for 10 minutes.

Add the prawns, fish and bamboo shoots and simmer for a further 4 minutes. Add the tomatoes and lime juice and check the seasoning, adding more fish sauce and sugar, if necessary.

Remove and discard the lemon grass stalks, then divide the soup between six bowls and scatter over the coriander and basil leaves.

CORN FRITTERS

Ingredients

Serves 4

3 spring onions, chopped finely

325 g/11½ oz canned sweetcorn kernels, drained

1 red pepper, deseeded and finely chopped

small handful of fresh coriander, chopped

2 garlic cloves, crushed

2 eggs

2 tsp caster sugar

1 tbsp fish sauce

2 tbsp rice flour or cornflour

vegetable or groundnut oil, for shallow-frying

dip

2 red peppers, deseeded and halved

2 tomatoes, peeled, deseeded and coarsely chopped

1 tbsp vegetable or groundnut oil, for shallow-frying

1 onion, chopped

1 tbsp red curry paste

3–4 sprigs fresh coriander, chopped

Method

Combine all ingredients for the fritters in a bowl. Heat the oil in a frying pan and fry spoonfuls of the mixture, in batches, until golden brown on the underside. Flip over with a spatula to cook the second side. Remove from the frying pan, drain on kitchen paper and keep warm.

To make the dip, put the red peppers on a baking sheet and place, skin side up, under a hot grill, until blackened. Using tongs, transfer to a plastic bag, tie the top and leave to cool slightly.

When the peppers are cool enough to handle, peel off the skins and chop the flesh. Put into a blender or food processor with the tomatoes and process until smooth.

Heat the oil in a heavy-based saucepan and cook the onion and curry paste for 3–4 minutes, until softened. Add the pepper and tomato purée and cook gently until tender and hot. Stir in the chopped coriander, cook for 1 minute, and serve hot with the fritters.

WONTONS

Ingredients

Serves 4

filling

2 tbsp vegetable or groundnut oil

6 spring onions, chopped

125 g/4½ oz mushrooms, chopped

55 g/2 oz fine French beans, chopped

55 g/2 oz sweetcorn kernels, drained if canned

1 egg, beaten

3 tbsp Thai soy sauce

1 tbsp palm sugar or soft, light brown sugar

½ tsp salt

wontons

24 wonton wrappers

1 egg, beaten

vegetable or groundnut oil, for deep-frying

Method

To make the filling, heat the oil in a preheated wok and stir-fry the spring onions, mushrooms and beans for 1–2 minutes, until softened. Add the sweetcorn, stir well to mix and then push the vegetables to the side. Pour in the egg. Stir until lightly set before incorporating the vegetables and adding the soy sauce, sugar and salt. Remove the wok from the heat.

Place the wonton wrappers in a pile on a work surface. Put a teaspoonful of the filling in the centre of the top wrapper. Brush the edges with beaten egg and fold in half diagonally to make a small triangular parcel. Repeat with the remaining wrappers and filling.

Heat the oil for deep-frying in a wok or large frying pan. Add the parcels, in batches, and deep-fry for 3–4 minutes, until golden brown. Remove from the wok with a slotted spoon and drain on kitchen paper. Keep warm while you cook the remaining wontons. Serve hot.

GREEN CHICKEN CURRY

Method

Heat the oil in a wok or large frying pan and stir-fry the onion and garlic for 1–2 minutes, until starting to soften. Add the curry paste and stir-fry for 1–2 minutes.

Add the coconut milk, stock and lime leaves, bring to the boil and add the chicken. Lower the heat and simmer gently for 15–20 minutes, until the chicken is tender.

Add the fish sauce, soy sauce, lime rind and juice and sugar. Cook for 2–3 minutes, until the sugar has dissolved. Serve immediately, garnished with chopped coriander.

Ingredients

Serves 4

1 tbsp vegetable or groundnut oil

1 onion, sliced

1 garlic clove, finely chopped

2–3 tbsp Thai green curry paste

400 ml/14 fl oz coconut milk

150 ml/5 fl oz chicken stock

4 kaffir lime leaves

4 skinned, boned chicken breasts, cut into cubes

1 tbsp fish sauce

2 tbsp Thai soy sauce

grated rind and juice of ½ lime

1 tsp palm sugar or soft, light brown sugar

4 tbsp chopped fresh coriander, to garnish

MONKFISH AND LIME with CHILLI SAUCE

Ingredients

Serves 4

4 x 115 g/4 oz monkfish fillets

25 g/1 oz rice flour or cornflour

6 tbsp vegetable or groundnut oil

4 garlic cloves, crushed

2 large fresh red chillies, deseeded and sliced

2 tsp palm sugar or soft, light brown sugar

juice of 2 limes

grated rind of 1 lime

boiled rice, to serve

Method

Toss the fish in the flour, shaking off any excess. Heat the oil in a wok and fry the fish on all sides until browned and cooked through, taking care when turning not to break it up.

Lift the fish out of the wok and keep warm. Add the garlic and chillies and stir-fry for 1–2 minutes, until they have softened.

Add the sugar, the lime juice and rind and 2–3 tablespoons of water and bring to the boil. Simmer gently for 1–2 minutes, then spoon the mixture over the fish. Serve immediately with rice.

CRISPY PORK DUMPLINGS

Ingredients

Serves 4

350 g/12 oz minced pork

2 tbsp finely chopped fresh coriander

1 garlic clove, crushed

1 fresh green chilli, deseeded and chopped

3 tbsp cornflour

1 egg white

½ tsp salt

16 wonton wrappers

1 tbsp water

vegetable or groundnut oil, for frying

chilli sauce, to serve

Method

Put the pork in a bowl and beat in the coriander, garlic, chilli, 1 tablespoon of the cornflour, the egg white and salt. Beat together to a thick, smooth texture. With damp hands shape into 16 equal portions and roll into balls.

Put a pork ball in the centre of each wonton wrapper. Make a paste by mixing the remaining cornflour with 1 tablespoon of water. Brush the edges of the wrappers with the cornflour paste and gather them up around the filling to make half into small, sack-like parcels, and the rest into triangular shapes.

Arrange the dumplings in a single layer (in batches if need be) in the top of a steamer and cook over boiling water for 10–15 minutes, until the meat is cooked through.

Heat the oil in a wok or large frying pan and carefully drop the parcels into it. Deep-fry for 2–3 minutes, until golden brown and crisp. Drain on kitchen paper and serve hot with chilli sauce.

SPICY BEEF WITH POTATO

Method

Cut the beef into thick slices and place in a shallow dish. Put the soy sauce, fish sauce, 1 tablespoon of the oil, the coriander roots, peppercorns, garlic and sugar in a food processor and process to a thick paste. Scrape the paste into the dish and toss the beef to coat. Cover with clingfilm and set aside to marinate in the fridge for at least 3 hours, preferably overnight.

Heat the remaining oil in a wok. Lift the beef out of the marinade, reserving the marinade, and fry for 3–4 minutes on each side, until browned. Add the reserved marinade and the potatoes with the measured water and gradually bring to the boil. Simmer for 6–8 minutes, or until the potatoes are tender.

Add the spring onions and spinach. Cook gently until the greens have wilted. Serve immediately with rice or noodles.

Ingredients

Serves 4–6

450 g/1 lb beef fillet

2 tbsp Thai soy sauce

2 tbsp fish sauce

2 tbsp vegetable or groundnut oil

3–4 coriander roots, chopped

1 tbsp crushed black peppercorns

2 garlic cloves, chopped

1 tbsp palm sugar or soft, light brown sugar

350 g/12 oz potatoes, diced

150 ml/5 fl oz water

bunch of spring onions, chopped

225 g/8 oz baby spinach leaves

cooked rice or noodles, to serve

SPICY RICE PUDDING

Ingredients

Serves 6

400 ml/14 fl oz canned coconut milk

150 ml/5 fl oz milk

55 g/2 oz soft brown sugar

55 g/2 oz pudding rice

2 tsp mixed spice

25 g/1 oz butter

1 tsp ground cinnamon

Method

Pour the coconut milk and milk into a saucepan and heat gently. Add the sugar and stir until it has dissolved.

Add the rice and spice and gradually bring to the boil. Simmer gently, stirring frequently, for 45–60 minutes, until thickened.

Stir in the butter and, once it has melted, serve immediately, sprinkled with cinnamon.

PINEAPPLE AND LIME SORBET

Ingredients

Serves 4

225 g/8 oz caster sugar

600 ml/1 pint water

grated rind and juice of 2 limes

1 small pineapple, peeled, quartered and chopped

sweet biscuits, to serve

Method

Put the sugar and water into a saucepan and heat gently, stirring until the sugar has dissolved. Bring to the boil and simmer for 10 minutes.

Stir in the grated rind of the lime and half the juice. Remove from the heat and leave to cool.

Put the pineapple in a blender or food processor and process until smooth. Add to the cold syrup with the remaining lime juice. Pour into a freezerproof container and freeze until crystals have formed around the edge.

Turn out the sorbet into a bowl. Beat well with a fork to break up the crystals. Return to the freezer and chill overnight. Serve with sweet biscuits.

GRILLED BANANAS

Method

Put the creamed coconut and double cream in a small saucepan and heat gently until the coconut has dissolved. Remove from the heat and set aside to cool for 10 minutes, then whisk until thick but floppy.

Peel the bananas and toss in the lime juice and rind. Lightly oil a preheated griddle pan and cook the bananas, turning once, for 2–3 minutes, until soft and browned.

Toast the dry unsweetened coconut on a piece of foil under a grill until lightly browned. Sprinkle the bananas with the toasted coconut and serve with the coconut cream.

Ingredients

Serves 4

55 g/2 oz block creamed coconut, chopped

150 ml/5 fl oz double cream

4 bananas

juice and rind of 1 lime

1 tbsp vegetable or peanut oil

50 g/1¾ oz dry unsweetened coconut

Melbourne

Melbourne's food culture offers great variety with a real enjoyment of upmarket, trendy and simple dining. A food revolution has swept through Australia in the past couple of decades, but the country's second city has steadfastly maintained its reputation as the top food city. The chefs have always been known for their sophisticated style, and their enthusiasm for embracing the ingredients and flavours brought by Asian, Greek and Middle Eastern immigrants has resulted in what's known as Mod Oz cooking – try Lightly Seared Kangaroo on Polenta for an example of this contemporary, fusion-style of food. Barbecuing never goes out of fashion, and Empire favourites from England, such as Sticky Date Pudding and Apple & Rhubarb Crumble, remain popular with the city's discerning diners.

Salt & Pepper Squid

Ingredients

Serves 4

2 tsp coarse sea salt

½ tsp Sichuan or black peppercorns

400 g/14 oz cleaned squid bodies, tentacles removed and bodies cut into 1-cm/½-inch rings

about 2 tbsp cornflour

sunflower oil or groundnut oil, for frying

½ tbsp very finely chopped fresh parsley (optional)

4 Webbs lettuce or radicchio leaf cups and lemon wedges, to serve

Method

Put the salt in a mortar and grind with a pestle. Add the peppercorns, pound to crush them lightly and grind until both seasonings are very fine, then set aside. Meanwhile, bring a large saucepan of water to the boil.

Drop the squid rings into the boiling water and cook for 15 seconds. They will form loops and lose their translucent whiteness. Do not overcook. Drain and refresh under cold running water. Shake dry, then tip onto a clean tea towel and pat dry. Put the cornflour on a plate.

Heat 5 cm/2 inches of the oil in a wok or deep frying pan to 180°C/350°F, or until a cube of bread browns in 30 seconds. Dredge half the squid rings in the cornflour and shake off the excess. Drop them in the oil and fry for 20 seconds. Use a slotted spoon to remove them from the oil and drain on folded kitchen paper. Return the oil to the correct temperature and cook the remaining squid rings.

Sprinkle the hot squid rings with the salt-and-pepper mixture to taste and add parsley, if using, for colour. Toss to distribute the seasoning, then divide between the lettuce cups. Serve at once with lemon wedges on the side for squeezing over. Any leftover seasoning mixture will keep in an airtight container in a cupboard for several months.

Pear, Rocket & Blue Cheese Salad with Balsamic Vinaigrette

Method

To make the dressing, put the oil, vinegar, and salt and pepper to taste in a large bowl and whisk until blended and thickened. Cover and set aside.

Just before serving, quarter, core and thinly slice the pear, adding it to the bowl with the dressing as it is prepared, then gently toss so all the pieces are coated with dressing. Add the rocket and cheese and toss again to combine. Sprinkle over the pine kernels and serve.

Ingredients

Serves 4–6

1 dessert pear, such as Bosc

2 bunches wild rocket, rinsed and shaken dry

85 g/3 oz blue cheese, such as Gorgonzola, crumbled

3 tbsp pine kernels, toasted

dressing

4 tbsp extra virgin olive oil

1 tbsp balsamic vinegar

salt and pepper

Bruschetta with Vine-Ripened Tomatoes, Basil & Olive Oil

Ingredients

Makes 8

4 firm vine-ripened plum tomatoes, peeled, cored, deseeded and finely chopped

8 slices ciabatta, about 1 cm/½ inch thick

good fruity olive oil

2 or 3 large garlic cloves, halved

sea salt

basil leaves, to garnish

Method

Put the tomatoes in a nylon sieve over a bowl, sprinkle with salt and leave to drain. Meanwhile, preheat the grill to high with the grill rack positioned 10 cm/4 inches from the heat.

Brush both sides of the bread slices with olive oil. Place on the rack and grill for 2 minutes, or until crisp and lightly browned, then turn and grill on the other side. Remove the toast from the heat and rub one side of each slice with the garlic, pressing down firmly.

Shake the sieve to remove any moisture from the tomatoes, then divide them between the toasts. Drizzle with a little more olive oil and scatter basil leaves over, then serve.

Lightly-Seared Kangaroo on Polenta

Method

Preheat the oven to 110°C/225°F/Gas Mark ¼. Bring 800 ml/1½ pints water to the boil in a large saucepan. Melt 15 g/½ oz of the butter with the oil in a large frying pan over a medium heat. Add the onions and fry, stirring occasionally, for 3 minutes. Add the garlic and continue stirring for 2 minutes, or until the onions are soft and browned. Use a slotted spoon to remove the onions from the pan and keep warm in the preheated oven.

Add a little oil to the pan, if necessary. Season the steaks with salt and pepper on both sides, then add to the pan over a medium–high heat and fry for 3 minutes. Turn the steaks over and fry for a further 3 minutes for medium or 4–5 minutes for well done. Remove from the pan, add to the onions and keep warm.

Add the wine and rosemary to the pan and bring to the boil, scraping the pan with a wooden spoon. Season with salt and pepper and leave to bubble until reduced by about half.

Meanwhile, add the polenta and ½ teaspoon salt to the boiling water in a steady stream, stirring, and boil for 1 minute, or according to the packet instructions, until thickened and soft. Add salt and pepper to taste.

Pour any juices from the onions and kangaroo into the bubbling wine and adjust the seasoning, if necessary. Transfer the steaks to warmed plates, strain the wine into a small jug and pour over, then add a mound of polenta.

Ingredients

Serves 4

85 g/3 oz butter

2 tbsp olive oil, plus extra if needed, for frying

2 large onions, thinly sliced

2 garlic cloves, crushed

4 kangaroo fillet steaks, about 125 g/4½ oz each and 2.5 cm/1 inch thick

300 ml/10 fl oz dry red wine, such as Shiraz

sprig of fresh rosemary

200 g/7 oz quick-cook polenta

salt and pepper

Seared Tuna with Green Olive Dressing

Method

Up to a day before cooking, put all the ingredients for the dressing in a non-metallic bowl, adding the chilli, if using, and salt and pepper to taste, then cover and set aside until required.

When ready to cook, heat a large dry cast-iron ridged griddle pan over a very high heat until a splash of water 'dances' on the surface. Brush one surface of each tuna steak with oil from the dressing, then place oiled-side down on the griddle and cook for 2 minutes.

Brush the top of the steaks with more oil from the dressing, then, using tongs, flip the steaks over, season to taste with salt and pepper and continue cooking a further 30 seconds for rare or up to 2 minutes for well done.

Transfer the steaks to plates and spoon a little of the dressing over each. Serve the remaining dressing separately, along with plenty of bread to mop up the rich oil.

Ingredients

Serves 4

4 tuna steaks, about 150 g/5½ oz each and 1 cm/½ in thick

sea salt and pepper

crusty bread, to serve

dressing

250 ml/9 fl oz garlic-flavoured olive oil

200 g/7 oz meaty stoned green olives, chopped

4 anchovy fillets in olive oil, chopped

4 tbsp fresh orange juice

finely grated rind of 1 large orange

½ tsp ground cumin

½ tsp ground coriander

squeeze of lemon juice

1 fresh red chilli, deseeded and finely chopped, or to taste (optional)

salt and pepper

Barbecued-Asian-Flavoured Poussins

Method

To make the marinade, mix all the ingredients together in a non-metallic bowl large enough to hold both poussins, then set aside.

Ease the skin from the breast flesh on both birds. Gently slide the orange slices under the skin, then ease the skin back over the slices. Put the poussins in the marinade and rub the mixture all over. Cover with clingfilm and leave to marinate in the fridge for 4–24 hours, turning occasionally.

Remove the poussins from the fridge 20 minutes in advance of cooking.

Heat the barbecue. Brush the rack with olive oil and position it about 10 cm/4 inches above the heat. Spear each poussin with two long metal skewers, from left to right at the top and bottom, to keep them flat. Put the birds on the grill rack, breast-side down, and grill for 20–25 minutes on each side, basting occasionally with the remaining marinade, until the juices run clear when the thighs are pierced.

Leave to rest for 10 minutes, then cut each bird in half and remove the orange slices.

Alternatively, preheat the oven to 180°C/350°F/Gas Mark 4. Heat a large ridged cast-iron griddle pan over a high heat until a splash of water 'dances' on the surface. Brush with olive oil, then add the unskewered birds and griddle for 10 minutes, or until browned. Turn the birds over and put the pan in the preheated oven for a further 30 minutes, basting occasionally with the remaining marinade, until the juices run clear when the thighs are pierced.

Meanwhile, mix the olive oil, orange juice and sesame oil with salt and pepper to taste in a non-metallic bowl. Add the watercress, pepper and sesame seeds and toss together.

Arrange a portion of salad on each plate and serve with half a poussin on top. Sprinkle with coriander and serve hot or at room temperature.

Ingredients

Serves 4

2 poussins, about 450 g/1 lb each, spatchcocked

1 orange, thinly sliced

4 tbsp extra virgin olive oil, plus extra for oiling

1½ tbsp fresh orange juice

1 tsp sesame oil

400 g/14 oz fresh watercress leaves, trimmed, rinsed and thoroughly dried

1 red pepper, cored, deseeded and thinly shredded with a vegetable peeler

2 tbsp sesame seeds, toasted

salt and pepper

chopped fresh coriander, to garnish

marinade

6 tbsp sunflower oil

4 tbsp soy sauce

2 tbsp sesame oil

2 garlic cloves, very finely chopped

1-cm/½-inch piece fresh ginger, grated

pinch chilli flakes, to taste

Marinated Rack of Lamb with Warm Tomato, Bean & Herb Salad

Ingredients

Serves 3–4

2 racks of lamb with 6 ribs each, chine bones removed

salt and pepper

marinade

4 garlic cloves, crushed

4 tbsp extra virgin olive oil

4 tbsp white wine vinegar

1 tbsp smooth mustard, such as Dijon

1 tbsp clear honey

1 tsp fresh oregano leaves

1 tsp fresh thyme leaves

salad

4 tbsp olive oil

2 large tomatoes, halved, cored and coarsely chopped

2 large garlic cloves, finely chopped

400 g/14 oz canned cannellini beans or butter beans, drained and rinsed

4 spring onions, trimmed and finely chopped

1 large peeled red pepper in oil, drained and sliced

2 tbsp chopped fresh parsley

2 tbsp chopped fresh mint

squeeze of lemon juice (optional)

salt and pepper

fresh basil leaves, to garnish

Method

To make the marinade, put all the ingredients in a polythene bag. Hold closed and shake to blend the ingredients. Add the racks of lamb, re-seal and shake again. Leave to marinate in the fridge for 4–24 hours, shaking occasionally. Remove from the fridge 20 minutes before cooking. Preheat the oven to 200°C/400°F/Gas Mark 6.

When ready to cook, remove the meat from the marinade, scrape off the herbs and pat dry. Place in a roasting tin and sprinkle the fatty surface with salt and pepper. Put the tin in the preheated oven and roast for 25 minutes per 500 g/1 lb 2 oz plus 15 minutes for medium or 30 minutes per 500 g/ 1 lb 2 oz plus 15 minutes for well done. Remove from the oven and leave to rest for 10 minutes before cutting into individual cutlets.

Meanwhile, to make the salad, heat the oil in a large frying pan over a medium heat. Add the tomatoes and garlic and stir for 3 minutes, or until the tomatoes soften and start to break down. Stir in the beans, spring onions, red pepper, parsley, mint, and salt and pepper to taste. Stir until all the ingredients are warmed through, then remove from the heat. Add a squeeze of lemon juice, if using, and adjust the seasoning.

Divide into cutlets and arrange on plates with the warm salad spooned over. Scatter the salad with basil leaves just before serving.

Rhubarb & Apple Crumble

Ingredients

Serves 4–6

450 g/1 lb rhubarb, cut into 5-cm/1-inch pieces

3 large apples, such as Granny Smiths, peeled, cored and chopped

2 tbsp orange juice or apple juice

4 tbsp soft light brown sugar

55 g/2 oz butter, cut into pieces

4-cm/1½-inch piece fresh ginger

pouring cream, to serve

topping

175 g/6 oz plain flour

85 g/3 oz very cold butter, cut into pieces

85 g/3 oz caster sugar

2 tbsp rolled oats

Method

Heat the oven to 190°C/375°F/Gas Mark 5 and lightly grease a 1.2-litre/2-pint ovenproof serving dish.

Put the rhubarb, apples, orange juice and sugar in the dish and mix together. Dot with butter and grate over the ginger.

To make the topping, put the flour in a large bowl and rub in the butter until the mixture forms large crumbs. Stir in the sugar and oats. Sprinkle the mixture over the filling, taking it right up to the edge of the dish.

Place the dish on a baking sheet and bake for 25–30 minutes until the topping is light brown, the filling is bubbling and the rhubarb and apples are tender when pierced with a fork. Leave to stand for 2 minutes, then serve with cream for pouring over.

Maple-Cream Tart

Ingredients

Makes 10–12 slices

375 g/13 oz ready-made shortcrust pastry, thawed if frozen

60 g/2¼ oz plain flour, plus extra for rolling the pastry

3 tbsp soft light brown sugar

700 ml/1¼ pints double cream

250 ml/9 fl oz pure maple syrup

2 eggs

4 tsp lemon juice

½ tsp salt

½ tsp ground nutmeg

2 tbsp icing sugar

Method

Preheat the oven to 200°C/400°F/Gas Mark 6. Roll out the pastry on a lightly floured surface and use to line a 23-cm/9-inch loose-based tart tin. Line the pastry with greaseproof paper and weigh down with dried beans. Place on a baking sheet and bake in the preheated oven for 15–20 minutes, until golden at the edges.

Meanwhile, combine the flour and sugar in a large bowl. Beat 450 ml/16 fl oz of the cream in another bowl with the maple syrup, eggs, lemon juice, salt and nutmeg. Slowly whisk this mixture into the flour, whisking until no lumps remain.

When the pastry case is golden, remove the paper and beans and reduce the oven temperature to 180°C/350°F/Gas Mark 4. Pour the filling into the pastry case, return to the oven and cook for 30–35 minutes, until set. Remove the tart from the oven and leave to cool completely on a wire rack.

Whip the remaining cream until soft peaks form. Sift over the icing sugar and continue whipping until stiff. Just before serving, spread the whipped cream over the surface of the tart. Cut into slices to serve.

Sticky Date Puddings

Method

Preheat the oven to 180°C/350°F/Gas Mark 4. Grease four 175-ml/6-fl oz pudding basins or ramekins and dust with flour. Line the bases with greaseproof paper and grease the paper.

Beat the butter and sugar until creamed and light. Beat in the eggs, one at a time. Stir in the vanilla extract. Sift over the flour, baking powder and salt and beat in. Slowly add the milk until the mixture has a soft dropping consistency: you might not need it all. Fold in the dates. Spoon the mixture into the moulds, filling them three-quarters full.

Place the moulds in a roasting tin and pour in enough boiling water to come halfway up the sides of the moulds. Bake in the preheated oven for 40–45 minutes until set and a skewer inserted in the centre of the puddings comes out clean. Remove the moulds from the tin and leave to stand for 2 minutes before turning out onto individual plates.

Meanwhile, to make the sauce, put the cream, sugar and vanilla in a saucepan over a medium–high heat, stirring until the sugar melts. Bring to the boil and boil for 5 minutes. Stir in the nuts. Spoon the hot sauce over the puddings and serve at once, with a scoop of ice cream on top.

Ingredients

Serves 4

90 g/3½ oz butter, softened, plus extra for greasing

90 g/3½ oz dark muscovado sugar

3 eggs

½ tsp vanilla extract

90 g/3½ oz self-raising flour, plus extra for dusting

¼ tsp baking powder

pinch of salt

about 2 tbsp milk

115 g/4 oz stoned dates, coarsely chopped and tossed with 1 tbsp plain flour

good quality vanilla ice cream, to serve

caramel pecan sauce

75 ml/2½ fl oz double cream

40 g/1½ oz dark muscovado sugar

40 g/1½ oz soft light brown sugar

¾ tsp vanilla extract

4 tbsp chopped pecan nuts

Index